**NEW YORK REVIEW BOOKS**
CLASSICS

# NOVELS IN THREE LINES

FÉLIX FÉNÉON (1861–1944) was born in Turin (his father was a traveling salesman), raised in Burgundy, and came to Paris after placing first in a competitive exam for jobs in the War Office. He was employed as a clerk there for thirteen years, rising to chief clerk, and was considered a model employee. During this time he also edited the work of Rimbaud and Lautréamont, reviewed books and art (he helped to discover Georges Seurat), and was a regular at Mallarmé's Tuesday evening salon. Fénéon was active too in anarchist circles, and in 1894, after the bombing of a restaurant popular among politicians and financiers and the assassination by an Italian anarchist of the French president, he and twenty-nine others were arrested on suspicion of conspiracy—though in the subsequent so-called Trial of the Thirty Fénéon and most of his co-defendants were easily acquitted. Soon after, Fénéon became the editor of the *Revue Blanche*, where he featured Debussy as his music critic and André Gide as his book critic and published Proust, Apollinaire, and Jarry, as well as his own translation of Jane Austen's *Northanger Abbey*. After the *Revue Blanche* folded, Fénéon went to work as a journalist, first for the conservative *Le Figaro*, then, starting in 1906, for the liberal broadsheet *Le Matin*, for which he composed the pieces collected in *Novels in Three Lines*. In later life Fénéon sold paintings at the Bernheim-Jeune gallery and for a while ran his own publishing house. In response to a proposal to publish a collection of his own work, he remarked, "I aspire only to silence."

LUC SANTE is the author of *Low Life*, *Evidence*, *The Factory of Facts*, and, most recently, *Kill All Your Darlings: Pieces 1990–2005*. He is a frequent contributor to *The New York Review of Books* and teaches writing and the history of photography at Bard College.

# NOVELS
# IN
# THREE LINES

## FÉLIX FÉNÉON

Translated and with an Introduction by
LUC SANTE

 NEW YORK REVIEW BOOKS

*New York*

This is a New York Review Book
Published by The New York Review of Books
1755 Broadway, New York, NY 10019
www.nyrb.com

Library of Congress Cataloging-in-Publication Data
Fénéon, Félix, 1861–1944.
  [Nouvelles en trois lignes. English]
  Novels in three lines / by Félix Fénéon ; translated and with an introduction by
Luc Sante.
      p. cm. — (New York Review Books Classics)
  ISBN-13: 978-1-59017-230-8 (alk. paper)
  ISBN-10: 1-59017-230-2 (alk. paper)
  I. Sante, Luc.  II. Title.
PQ2611.E565N613 2007
843'.912—dc22

                              2007014634


ISBN 978-1-59017-230-8


Printed in the United States of America on acid-free paper.
10 9 8 7 6 5 4 3

catastrophe. C'est donc que le renverse-
[...] de l'aération, à propos duquel les in-
[...]ieurs de l'Etat furent incriminés, n'a
[...]sé la mort d'aucun survivant.

## [C]ONSEIL DES MINISTRES RAMBOLITAIN

[...]u *Figaro* :

[...]'est aujourd'hui la première fois que le
[...]seil des ministres actuel aura tenu séance
[...] Rambouillet, et la première fois aussi que
[...] Fallières aura à recevoir les ministres du
[...]vernement dans la majestueuse et estivale
[...]neure.

[...]ais il y a des traditions.

[...]es ministres arriveront le matin vers dix
[...]res et ils se réuniront immédiatement en
[...]seil. La séance durera jusqu'à midi et
[...]mi pour reprendre ensuite à deux heures.
[...] président a invité, en effet, les membres
[...] cabinet à déjeuner, afin de leur permet-
[...] d'épuiser, dans cette journée, toutes les
[...]aires auxquelles il est indispensable qu'ils
[...]nnent une solution avant de partir en va-
[...]ces. C'est donc seulement vers cinq ou six
[...]res du soir que prendra fin, vraisembla-
[...]ment, le conseil où sera réglée notamment
[...] question de l'assistance obligatoire aux
[...]llards qui n'a pas été, comme on l'a vu,
[...]s soulever, ces jours-ci, d'assez sérieuses
[...]ficultés.

[...]. Clemenceau fera signer également le
[...]uvement administratif dont nous avons
[...] fait connaître les principales disposi-
[...]ns.

[...]e soir, pour dîner, les ministres seront
[...]trés à Paris, et, dès le lendemain, la plu-
[...] d'entre eux prendront leur villégiature,
[...]nsportant. comme tous les ans à pareille
[...]que, le siège du gouvernement vers la
[...]ntagne ou vers la mer...

## EN DESCENDANT DU TRAIN

[...]u *Petit Parisien* :

[...]me Blanche-Ernestine Gaillard, âgée de
[...]gt-neuf ans, domiciliée allée Got, à Fran-
[...]ville, venait de descendre d'un train, à la
[...]re du Nord, et de s'engager dans la rue de
[...]nkerque lorsque tout à coup elle poussa
[...] cri d'effroi et se jeta de côté. Devant elle
[...] tenait un homme dont le visage exprimait
[...] plus violente colère. Il brandissait un re-
[...]ver en vociférant :

— Ah ! misérable ! je savais bien que je
[...] retrouverais... L'heure de la vengeance a
[...]in sonné ! ce n'est pas trop tôt !

[...] fin de la phrase fut coupée par une sé-
[...] de détonations et les nombreux prome-
[...]urs, témoins de cette scène tragique, virent
[...] malheureuse femme s'abîmer sur le sol :
[...]ux balles tirées à bout portant venaient de
[...] teindre en pleine poitrine.

[...]mmédiatement arrêté et quelque peu mal-
[...]né par la foule indignée, le meurtrier fut
[...]né au commissariat du quartier, où il fut,
[...]s tarder, introduit dans le bureau de M.
[...]her.

[...] déclara se nommer Charles Piedson, être
[...] de vingt-trois ans, employé de commerce,
[...] Saint-Denis.

[...]près avoir vécu, durant plusieurs mois,
[...]c Mme Gaillard, il avait été brusquement
[...]ndonné par cette personne, qui s'était ré-
[...]iée dans une petite propriété qu'elle possé-
[...] à Franconville.

[...] a été envoyé au dépôt. Mme Blanche-Er-
[...]stine Gaillard, dont l'état est des plus alar-

---

On évitera peut-être le débat devant [...]
[...]ges ; on n'éludera pas le jugement de l'op[...]

## NOUVELLES EN TROIS LIG[...]

### BANLIEUE PARISIENNE

— M. Dupuis, miroitier à Paris, et M[...]
chand ont été blessés, à Versailles, da[...]
accident d'auto. Le chauffeur Girard [...]

— Les cartouches de la bombe d'Arge[...]
proviennent d'un militaire en activité [...]
été volés dans une poudrière.

### DÉPARTEMENTS

— Une jeune fille, Louise Azéma, a reç[...]
le ventre une balle émanant d'un obus [...]
du camp du Causse, près Castres. (*Ha[...]*

— Les fermiers de S.-et-M. proposen[...]
ouvriers agricoles 3 fr. et 3 fr. 75 par [...]
suivant le mois. (*Par téléphone.*)

— Nuitamment, volets et vitres ont é[...]
sés chez 3 grévistes de Lochrist (Morb[...]
Le mouvement de rentrée s'accentue.

— D'adjoint au maire de Saint-Etien[...]
socialiste Plantevin devient ce maire [...]
voix. Il remplace M. Ledin, élu député.

— Dans le lac d'Annecy, trois jeunes [...]
nageaient. L'un, Janinetti, disparut. Plo[...]
des autres. Ils le ramenèrent, mais mort.

— Le radicalisme gagne un siège au c[...]
général du Rhône, grâce à l'élection [...]
Bernard par le canton de Villefranche.

— Bien des Dunkerquois sont morts [...]
guerre. Leur monument s'inaugurait hie[...]
la présidence Guillain et Trystram. (*D[...]*

— Nény, Pruvost père et fils et autres [...]
capés » de Courrières sont partis pour [...]
remercier les sauveteurs westphaliens.

— A Verlinghem (Nord), Mme Ridez, 3[...]
a été égorgée par un voleur, cependan[...]
son mari était à la messe. (*Havas.*)

— Les tisseurs de Ramonchamp (Vosge[...]
tiennent le maintien au tarif ancien, qu[...]
laient modifier les patrons. Leur grève ce[...]

### ÉTRANGER

— Le roi et la reine d'Espagne quit[...]
Santander aujourd'hui à 3 h. de l'après[...]
pour l'Angleterre, à bord de la *Giralda*.

— La Porte a nommé M. Constantin [...]
theodory membre de la commission des [...]
tionnaires civils prince de Samos. (*Hav[...]*

— Une grande fête a été donnée à [...]
neiro, en l'honneur de M. Root, minist[...]
affaires étrangères des Etats-Unis. (*Hav[...]*

— A Constantinople. les douaniers o[...]
avertis que l'augmentation des droits d[...]
sera appliquée à partir du 1er septembre[...]

— Les navires anglais *Kilmore* et *Mo[...]*
*ma* sont entrés en collision près West-[...]
L'un coula et l'autre fut endommagé.

— Victor-Emmanuel III et la reine d[...]
Marguerite ont assisté à Rome à une c[...]
nie à la mémoire d'Humbert I[...]. (*Laffa[...]*

— Le steamer anglais *Castleford* s'est [...]
sur des rochers, près Falmouth (Angle[...]
Un remorqueur le ramena à Falmouth.

# INTRODUCTION

The original French title of this book, *Nouvelles en trois lignes*, can mean either "the news in three lines" or "novellas in three lines." It was the title under which these items— there are 1,220 of them in all; a mere 154 have been omitted here because their significance has fallen into obscurity —were all published in 1906 in the Paris daily newspaper *Le Matin*. Newspapers in many countries apart from the United States run columns of such brief stories, which in French are called *faits-divers* ("sundry events"; "fillers" are nearly but not quite the same—there is no simple English equivalent). They cover the same subjects as the rest of the paper—crime, politics, ceremony, catastrophe—but their individual narratives are compressed into a single frame, like photographs. They may suggest, portend, echo, pose questions, present enigmas, awaken troubling memories, but they usually do not have a second act. Cases in which a story runs over into a subsequent item on a later day are rare. People have been clipping and saving such items, for their oddity or their usually unintentional humor, since the *fait-divers* first made its appearance in the nineteenth century, but they have seldom if ever considered them literary texts, attributable to an author.

These, though, are all the work of one man, a great literary stylist who wrote little and published less, and who occupies a peculiar place in French cultural history. You might say that Félix Fénéon is invisibly famous: his name may ring a bell, and a number of his deeds are known and a few celebrated, but not many people could link the man with his accomplishments. Furthermore, he kept himself to himself. What we know of him is largely owed to the devotion of those around him. We know little, for example, about how he came to spend half the year 1906 composing unsigned three-line news items for a mass-circulation daily paper. The only reason we have them today is because Camille Plateel, his mistress for some fifty years, collected them in an album, which was found after both their deaths by Fénéon's literary executor, Jean Paulhan. Whatever Fénéon may have thought of them, he clearly did not stint on their composition. They are the poems and novels he never otherwise wrote, or at least did not publish or preserve. They demonstrate in miniature his epigrammatic flair, his exquisite timing, his pinpoint precision of language, his exceedingly dry humor, his calculated effrontery, his tenderness and cruelty, his contained outrage. His politics, his aesthetics, his curiosity and sympathy are all on view, albeit applied with tweezers and delineated with a single-hair brush. And they depict the France of 1906 in its full breadth, on a canvas of reduced scale but proportionate vastness. They might be considered Fénéon's *Human Comedy*.

# INTRODUCTION

Fénéon made it his business throughout his life (1861–1944) to remain behind the scenes, and in general he succeeded. He may have been somewhat more famous to his contemporaries than he is to us, but he was no less enigmatic. These days he is best known as the subject of a portrait by Paul Signac—which he disliked, and lamented for the rest of his days—in which he is shown in profile, proffering a lily, against a background of swirls and stars and patterns and colors that looks like early psychedelia. (It actually alludes to the theories of Charles Henry, a friend of both painter and subject, who sought a scientific basis for aesthetics.) Fénéon is as striking as the setting— very tall and very thin, with a goatish chin-beard that made people think of Uncle Sam: he was a "false Yankee," according to Apollinaire; "a satyr born in Brooklyn (U.S.A.)," according to Alfred Jarry; a "Yankee Mephistopheles," according to Remy de Gourmont.

His accomplishments all took place away from the lime-light, and were frequently in the service of others' work. He more or less discovered Georges Seurat, and had a great deal to do with his success and those of other Postimpressionists and Nabis: Signac, Pissarros père and fils, Maximilien Luce, Félix Vallotton, Toulouse-Lautrec, Bonnard, Vuillard, Maurice Denis. He edited Rimbaud's *Illuminations*—he was responsible for establishing the order of the sections, among other things—and produced the first public edition of Lautréamont's *Chants de Maldoror*. He founded several magazines and edited several more, including the *Revue blanche*, arguably the most important literary-artistic journal of its time (1893–1903). In later life he sold paintings at the

Bernheim-Jeune gallery and for a while ran his own publishing house, Éditions de la Sirène, where he published, among other things, the first French translation of James Joyce (*Dédale*, 1924).

He had a reputation as a literary stylist, although he never published a book in his lifetime, and a large number of his writings were anonymous or pseudonymous. In part this anonymity belonged to a longstanding literary tradition, and in part it was mere discretion, since Fénéon contributed to anarchist publications subject to scrutiny by the police. Fénéon's self-effacement went beyond the norm even for his time and milieu, however, and what we know of his personality suggests a number of possible reasons for this: a saturnine remoteness combined with an instinctual sense of noblesse oblige, a penchant for secrecy that attended both his love affairs and his acts of charity, a desire for the freedom afforded by disguise (he signed many of his letters under other names, too), perhaps also—although he never betrayed a hint of this—a dissatisfaction with his own talents in the light of the crowd of geniuses he frequented.

Everyone was awed by Fénéon, and he was beloved, too; his imposing silhouette, crackling intelligence, and severe wit were balanced by genuine compassion and generosity. The daunting shadow he cast can be measured by the assessment given after his death by the much younger André Breton, who was far less approachable to his own peers: "Although I got to know him, was amazed by him, admired and loved him, I never [fully] understood him.... His outer shell was rough, and slippery."[1] His biographer, Joan Ungersma Halperin,[2] notes that while Fénéon made a deep impression on everyone who knew him, that impression was subject to contradictions; one old friend claimed that he never laughed, another that his laughter could wake the dead. He seemed completely self-invented, from his appearance to his speech to his conduct. He wore no ornaments or jewelry of any kind; he made only infrequent, slight, "geometric" motions when he spoke; his face remained impassive and immobile at all times. Perhaps he was Baudelaire's dandy—self-contained, self-defined, answering to a code in which ethics and aesthetics are inextricably bound—made flesh.

Fénéon was born in Turin (his father was a traveling salesman), raised in Burgundy, and came to Paris as a result of placing first in a competitive exam, entered on a whim, for jobs in the War Office. He was employed as a clerk there for thirteen years, rising to chief clerk, and was considered a model employee. During this time he helped found the journals *La Libre revue*, *La Revue indépendante*, and *La Vogue*; reviewed books and art exhibitions; frequented the Symbolists and was a regular at Mallarmé's Tuesday

1. Letter to Jean Paulhan, 1949, quoted by Joan Ungersma Halperin, in *Félix Fénéon: Aesthete and Anarchist in Fin-de-Siècle Paris* (Yale University Press, 1988), p. 11. Maybe Breton's experience of Fénéon accounts for his otherwise unaccountable omission of the *Nouvelles en trois lignes* from the *Anthologie de l'humour noir* in its expanded editions of 1950 or 1966.
2. She also identified many of his unsigned or pseudonymous pieces and produced the most definitive edition of his work: *Oeuvres plus que complètes* (Geneva: Librairie Droz, 1970).

evening salon; wrote a few short stories and announced but never published an edition of Bossuet's sermons, as well as a novel he probably meant as a joke and never intended to write. He was also active in anarchist circles. Anarchism in France in the late nineteenth century was less a definite ideology than a spectrum of attitudes that hinged on a few common points: the heritage of the *enragés* in the Revolution, the example of Proudhon, the bitter memory of the Paris Commune and its bloody suppression, an affinity for Bakunin over Marx after the 1875 schism in the First International, a distrust of politics and a hatred of the military and the church. Sébastien Faure put it more simply: "The common point is the negation of the principle of Authority in social organization and a hatred of all the constraints imposed by the institutions that are based upon that principle."[3] The tendency otherwise ran the gamut from antiauthoritarian communism to libertarian individualism.

The two anarchist publications with which Fénéon was most involved present a striking contrast. *Le Père Peinard*, edited by Émile Pouget (who has been credited with coining the word "sabotage," and who later became a leading theorist of anarcho-syndicalism), was so determinedly populist that it was written entirely in workmen's slang, down to the masthead and the subscription blank. Fénéon contributed several accounts of large group painting shows in which he patiently explained, in that tongue, the workings and hierarchy of the arts in France to readers who could not

3. *Encyclopédie anarchiste*, quoted in *Ravachol et les anarchistes*, by Jean Maitron (Paris: Gallimard, 1964), p. 7.

be expected to know anything about it. (Note that as an anarchist Fénéon did not exhort or propagandize or indulge in apologias; rather, he exemplified anarchist conduct.) *L'Endehors*, on the other hand, was an elegant if generally unspecific expression of revolt, written and read by the literary and intellectual avant-garde. It was edited by Zo d'Axa (né Alphonse Galland), a flamboyant, rakishly bewhiskered free spirit who was dubbed "the musketeer" or "the patrician" of anarchy. When d'Axa, accused of sedition, was forced to flee to London in 1892, Fénéon silently took over the editor's chair.

But Fénéon's double life could not last. In the early 1890s a state of war existed between the anarchists and the government. On May Day 1891, the army fired on strikers and their families in the textile town of Fourmies, near the Belgian border; the same day a demonstration in the Paris suburb of Clichy turned into a gun battle between anarchists and police—which may well have been started by the police—after which two of the anarchists were given long prison sentences. To avenge both incidents, a man called Ravachol (né François Koenigstein) planted bombs at the Lobau barracks in Paris and at the homes of the two judges who pronounced sentence in the Clichy case. Although no one was injured, Ravachol was guillotined. After a lull, a series of reprisals ensued, which peaked in December 1893, when Auguste Vaillant tossed a bomb into the Chamber of Deputies, again with no injuries, not even interrupting the proceedings. At the guillotine, Vaillant predicted that his death would be avenged. A week later it was done: one person died and twenty were hurt when a bomb was thrown

into the Café Terminus near the Gare Saint-Lazare. The bomber was Émile Henry, a young friend of Fénéon's, a brilliant student whose militancy was exacerbated by the fate of his father, a former Communard who died of lead poisoning from working in Spanish mines during his exile. The Café Terminus bombing was significantly different from what had gone before because it targeted not specific antagonists but random petits bourgeois. The question divided anarchist opinion. The writer Octave Mirbeau declared that "A mortal enemy of anarchy could have acted no better than Émile Henry," while the poet Laurent Tailhade famously uttered, "*Qu'importent quelques vagues humanités si le geste est beau?*"[4]

Tailhade, with unimprovable irony, was the sole victim of the next major anarchist bombing. The cycle of deaths and reprisals would reach its logical culmination in June 1894, when Sadi Carnot, President of the Republic, was fatally stabbed by a visiting Italian anarchist. Before that, on April 4, a device was set on the windowsill of the restaurant of the Hôtel Foyot, across the street from the Palais du Luxembourg, meeting place of the Senate. Although the restaurant's clientele was composed primarily of politicians, financiers, and their mistresses, Tailhade, a recidivist gastronome, was an occasional visitor, and on that occasion was romancing his own mistress. He lost an eye in the blast. No one was ever formally accused; the case remained unsolved. Rumors flew, naturally, and a persistent one attached itself to Fénéon. It made its first appearance

4. "Of what importance are a few vague people if the gesture is beautiful?"

in print four years after his death, in Paulhan's preface to his edition of Fénéon's *Oeuvres*. Halperin goes farther and asserts that Fénéon confessed.[5] The evidence is a chain of hearsay, but suggestive. Halperin obtained the information, at one remove, from the poet André Salmon, who was half a generation younger than Fénéon but after 1900 traveled in the same circles. In *La Terreur noire*, his book on the French anarchists of the turn of the last century, Salmon wrote:

> Sixty-five years after the fact...a very old witness ...confided to me that a subtle man of letters had boasted to him at the time of having placed the bomb that exploded on the threshold of the Foyot. It is important to specify that this very well known man of letters, who is not forgotten even today, even though he wrote little, remained until the death of that poet...a great friend of Laurent Tailhade.[6]

Halperin's informant told her that the "old witness" was the Dutch émigré translator Alexandre Cohen, one of Fénéon's closest friends and equally active in anarchist activities (although he later followed the path of Charles Maurras to virulent right-wing nationalism, while Fénéon took the other road out, that of the Communist Party). Salmon's characterization of the culprit is unmistakably Fénéon. The word "subtle," the fact that he "wrote little"

5. Halperin, p. 276.
6. *La Terreur noire: Chronique du mouvement libertaire*, volume II (Paris: Jean-Jacques Pauvert, 1959), p. 95.

and yet remained unforgotten—the identification would have been clear to informed readers. It is of course possible that Salmon embellished or extrapolated, or that Cohen, who was ninety-five years old in 1959, was simply muddled—it may be significant that while Salmon writes that the boast occurred "*alors*," Cohen had been deported in 1893 and was living in London at the time. In view of the subsequent political split between him and Fénéon, he may even have sought some obscure belated payback.

Still, it would not be out of character for Fénéon to have done it. It is very difficult to pin Fénéon down, since he left behind few statements, much less self-revelations, and maintained a powerfully guarded personality. But he was fully committed to the cause, and furthermore had given Émile Henry one of his mother's dresses to use as a disguise when the latter delivered the bomb that blew up the police precinct house on Rue des Bons-Enfants in November 1892. The biggest sticking point in the Foyot bombing remains, as in the case of the Café Terminus, the choice of target: a public restaurant in which any number of innocent parties might have business. Salmon believed that the Foyot bomber had intended to blow up the Senate, but had been thwarted by the presence of guards, and had selected the Foyot as a last resort.

In any case, bombing was considered a legitimate tactic by quite a lot of people at the time. According to Hans Magnus Enzensberger:

> The hatred of the bourgeoisie was so enormous that
> all it took was the example of a single excuse for it to

discharge itself violently in the form of detonations of which kings and ministers were not the only victims: the bombs of the nameless terrorists who sought to tackle the big powers single-handedly exploded in theaters, luxury restaurants, and stock exchanges, in clubs and parliaments. In 1892 alone, there were registered in the United States 500 bombing attacks, and more than 1,000 in Europe.[7]

The tactical rationale was "propaganda by the deed," which could mean either that the masses would be inspired to follow spontaneously in revolt, or else that the consequent repression would be so severe that the populace would have no choice but to rise up against it. In truth, such reasoning was wishful—the real engine was rage. In the face of horrendous labor conditions, a vast and unbridgeable gap between rich and poor, minute surveillance of dissidents, and a draconian if capricious repression, the anarchists declared war on a power structure that was warring both against them and against the poor and unlettered who were in no position to fight back themselves. In court, after citing their tally of workaday murders by malnutrition, overwork, neglect, and exploitation, Émile Henry exhorted his opponents: "At least have the courage of your crimes, gentlemen of the bourgeoisie, and agree that our reprisals are fully legitimate."[8]

7. "Dreamers of the Absolute (Part II)," in *Politics and Crime* (New York: Seabury/ Continuum, 1974), p.78. Note, by contrast, that during an eighteen-month period in 1970 and 1971, there were 4,330 political bombings in the United States.
8. Halperin, p. 275.

Three weeks after the Foyot bombing, Fénéon was arrested in a sweep of anyone whose name could be connected to anarchist activities, a sweep that had been in progress since Ravachol's attacks but was now redoubled. (As Paulhan points out, however, it is significant that, considering the many prominent contributors to *L'Endehors*, Fénéon was the only literary figure to be arrested.) He was kept in prison for more than three months before the government figured out a case to mount against him and twenty-nine others, some of them in absentia, a range of defendants that mingled theorists and burglars, and included a butcher's apprentice accused of stealing a cutlet. Fénéon's arrest provoked considerable excitement on both sides. Much was made of his employment at the ministry, even more so after a search of his office (nothing was found in his apartment) turned up, in a coat closet, a vial of mercury and a matchbox containing eleven detonators. His friends rallied; the blameless Mallarmé said, in part, "You say they are talking of detonators. Certainly, for Fénéon, there are no better detonators than his articles."[9] When asked about the detonators in court, Fénéon claimed that his father, who had recently died, had found them in the street. The prosecutor suggested that such a find was rather unusual. Fénéon replied: "The examining magistrate asked me why I hadn't thrown them out the window instead of taking them to the Ministry. So you see, it is possible to find detonators in the street."[10] (They had, in fact,

9. Halperin, p. 282; from an article in *Le Soir*.
10. Jean Paulhan, "*F. F. ou le critique*," in Félix Fénéon, *Oeuvres* (Paris: Gallimard, 1948), p. 18–19.

belonged to Henry.) The Trial of the Thirty, as it was dubbed, was a show trial, staged during the August holidays, that produced nothing but good copy for the newspapers. Fénéon's wit made him the undisputed star. One day the judge received a package which proved to contain human feces. When he called for a recess to go wash his hands, Fénéon remarked to his lawyer in a stage whisper: "Not since Pontius Pilate has a judge washed his hands so ostentatiously."[11] Eventually the case foundered for lack of evidence, not to mention coherence, and although three burglars were convicted, all the anarchists were set free. Fénéon unsurprisingly lost his job, but the cultural impresario Thadée Natanson, who though he had never met Fénéon had provided him with his defense attorney, hired him to edit the *Revue blanche*.

Fénéon happily returned to obscurity. In the eight years he edited the *Revue blanche*, his name appeared in its pages only three times, to credit his translations of Poe's letters and Jane Austen's *Northanger Abbey*. "*Je n'aime que les travaux indirects*," he said. He invisibly determined the character of the journal, with his sensibility uniquely attuned to the present and the future. He published, among others, often very early in their careers, Proust, Apollinaire, Jarry, Paul Claudel, Charles Péguy, Jules Renard, Marcel Schwob, Maeterlinck, Verhaeren, Julien Benda, Léon Blum; Debussy was his music critic, André Gide his book critic. After 1900 he supplemented the aesthetic substance of the journal with serious studies of social questions and inter-

11. Paulhan, p. 20.

national affairs. In those years he himself wrote virtually nothing. *"Je n'aspire qu'au silence,"* he said to someone who offered to publish a collection of his work. Jarry called him *"celui qui silence,"* meaning both that he silences the non-sense of others and that he himself practices an active form of silence.[12] That would be the same silence that Rimbaud embodied when he abandoned poetry for Aden and Abyssinia, that Lautréamont enacted when he destroyed his *Poésies* and published only its preface, that Paul Valéry's Monsieur Teste exemplified by writing nothing at all. It is an aggressive silence, as charged, dense, and reverberating as Malevich's black canvas. It affirms that all writing is compromise, that conception will always trump execution, that ego and politics are everyone's coauthors. It may be rooted in despair but it grows in the direction of transcendence. It wishes to free poetry from books and release it into daily life.

After the *Revue blanche* folded—as is invariably the case with ambitious literary reviews, it did not recover its costs—Fénéon went to work as a journalist, first for the conservative institution *Le Figaro*. He mostly wrote anonymous copy, and only one byline of his has survived, in which he wondered whether there was any basis for the major panic of the day, the "yellow peril." (He interviewed Cesare Lombroso, Jules Verne, and the great geographer and anarchist Élisée Reclus, who suggested that the West was more immediately likely to exploit the population of China than to be invaded by it.) Early in 1906 he entered the

12. It is also a pun: *"celui qui s'y lance"* means "he who launches himself into [it]."

employ of *Le Matin*, a popular broadsheet of broadly liberal tenor, where after a few months he was assigned the *faits-divers* column on page 3, and he kept at it until November of that year, when he was hired by the Bernheim brothers to sell art in their gallery. He drew his news items from wire services, small-town newspapers, and direct communication from readers. He worked the evening or night shift, and wrote up to twenty of them daily, presumably in addition to other duties.

Given their ephemeral nature, Fénéon's items were not an object of public comment in their time, but their enduring impact is suggested by a 1914 entry in Apollinaire's anonymous *Mercure de France* column, *"La vie anecdotique"*:

> M. Félix Fénéon has never been very prodigal with his prose, and his conversation is rather laconic. Nevertheless, this writer so bare-bones that he so to speak invented, in his immortal three-line stories in *Le Matin*, the *words at liberty* adopted by the Futurists, has been silent for too long.[13]

Although the Futurists themselves did not acknowledge a debt to Fénéon for their *parole in libertà*, a glance at F. T. Marinetti's manifestos suggests a common essence: "Literature having up to now glorified thoughtful immobility, ecstasy, and slumber, we wish to exalt the aggressive movement, the feverish insomnia, running, the perilous leap, the

---

13. *Anecdotiques* (Paris: Gallimard, 1955), p. 151.

cuff, and the blow."[14] And if Fénéon did not exactly invent his form, he perfected it, streamlined it, gave it dynamism and tensile strength, made it an aggressive modernist vehicle. Halperin cites a few examples of entries from the column just before Fénéon took it over:

> The funeral of gendarme Refeveuille, killed by a burglar, took place yesterday, paid by the city of Evreux.

> In Brignoles, Mme. S., who had recently given birth, killed herself yesterday by jumping out a window, during a bout of fever.[15]

The inertness and complacency of these sentences is immediately evident when they are compared to Fénéon's:

> Again and again Mme Couderc, of Saint-Ouen, was prevented from hanging herself from her window bolt. Exasperated, she fled across the fields.

> There was a gas explosion at the home of Larrieux, in Bordeaux. He was injured. His mother-in-law's hair caught on fire. The ceiling caved in.

---

14. "The Foundation and Manifesto of Futurism," 1908. Contemporary English translation reprinted in *Theories of Modern Art*, edited by Herschel B. Chipp (Berkeley: University of California Press, 1968), p. 286. A 1914 drawing by Marinetti called *Words in Freedom* (*Chaudronneries*) shows a hodgepodge of signage and logotypes: gazomètres, moulins, sardines, guérit tout, etc.
15. Halperin, p. 355.

Fénéon, after all a disciple of Mallarmé, exercised his considerable talents for compression, distillation, and skeletal evocation, making the items something like haikai. He managed to engineer the most minimal, Swiss-watch examples of suspense (making them a special challenge for the translator, since word order is often crucial).

> Responding to a call at night, M. Sirvent, café owner of Caissargues, Gard, opened his window; a rifle shot destroyed his face.

He enjoyed combining thematically related items into double- or triple-deckers:

> Mme Fournier, M. Vouin, M. Septeuil, of Sucy, Tripleval, Septeuil, hanged themselves: neurasthenia, cancer, unemployment.

He constructed what can sound like short stories in concentrated tablet form:

> The schoolchildren of Niort were being crowned. The chandelier fell, and the laurels of three among them were spotted with a little blood.

> At five o'clock in the morning, M. P. Bouget was accosted by two men on Rue Fondary. One put out his right eye, the other his left. In Necker.

# INTRODUCTION

Sometimes it seems that the three lines can contain the substance of an entire novel:

> Eugène Périchot, of Pailles, near Saint-Maixent, entertained at his home Mme Lemartrier. Eugène Dupuis came to fetch her. They killed him. Love.

He made dry, glancing social commentary with little more than the verbal equivalent of a raised eyebrow:

> A dishwasher from Nancy, Vital Frérotte, who had just come back from Lourdes cured forever of tuberculosis, died Sunday by mistake.

> Finding his daughter, 19, insufficiently austere, Jallat, watchmaker of Saint-Étienne, killed her. It is true that he has eleven children left.

Occasionally an entry achieves the frozen perfection of an epigram:

> On the bowling lawn a stroke leveled M. André, 75, of Levallois. While his ball was still rolling he was no more.

As an art critic Fénéon had been noted for, among other things, the muted extravagance of his language. He drew vocabulary from the jargons of specialized professions, sciences, areas of study; horticultural and architectural and nautical terms, which his readers would usually have to look up or puzzle out, would repay that labor by their descriptive or metaphorical precision. Rather than being employed for show, such arcana provided a prophylaxis against the unanchored vagueness of most art criticism. Fénéon's language, enlisting the detachment and objectivity of science, partook of the same essence as the Pointillists' adamantine dots—so much like pixels—and Charles Henry's aesthetic theories, and the anarchists' invocations of Darwin and Huxley against authority and superstition. Now, writing for a mass audience, he could not count on his readers' using or even owning dictionaries, but his need for precision was no less. There may be few rare words in these stories, but there is not a word or a punctuation mark wasted. Translation can only go so far in attempting to convey Fénéon's virtuosic selection and ordering of words for nuance, rhythm, and maximum impact. Each item is a literary performance, just as each is nameless, evanescent, consumed in a instant and then used to wrap fish.

If each item is a miniature clockwork of language and event, the full thousand-and-some put together make a mosaic panorama. They represent the year 1906 in France, and they are charged with the essence of that time and place in a way that is routinely available to artifacts and impersonal documents while often remaining outside the grasp of literature. They testify to the growing importance and menace of the automobile, the medieval conditions that still prevailed in agriculture and country life, the often fortunate inefficiency of firearms, the vulnerability of rural populations to epidemic disease, the unflagging pomposity of the military establishment, the mutual suspicion and profound lack of understanding between the French and their colonial subjects, the increasing number of strikes and the unchangingly brutal state of factory labor, the continuing panic over the threat of anarchist bombs (twelve years of relative calm had gone by, while the next wave of anarchist violence, spearheaded by the Bonnot gang, lay five years in the future). It was the dead middle of the Third Republic, which stretched from the end of the Franco-Prussian War to the eve of World War II. Germany was, once again, a looming threat on the horizon, manifesting itself in that period mostly in the African colonies. The separation of church and state had been enacted the previous year, and much turmoil derived from the Catholic church's reduction in power and income, especially from its loss of the monopoly over primary education. It helps to know such things when reading the items, just as it helps to know that Sisowath was King of Cambodia, that revolution had almost broken out in Russia the year before, and that the writer Maurice Barrès (1862–1923), once an anarchist of the individualist persuasion, had become a very prominent blood-and-soil promoter of tradition. But such public matters occur just here and there. The stories represent daily life, after all, and so what is primarily visible is the range of human folly, greed, lust, rage as well as, very occasionally, love and kindness.

In 1906 the newspaper, around the world, was in its golden age. It enjoyed undisputed dominion over communication (radio would not come about for another decade and a half; movies and sound recordings were still in a primitive state), it existed in profusion (major cities would have from four or five to a dozen or more competing morning papers, and an only slightly smaller number of evening editions), and attempts to increase circulation resulted in gimmicks and experiments that were often trivial but sometimes ambitious and transformative (color comics sections, rotogravure supplements, graphics that broke across the column format). At the same time, just-the-facts impersonality had not yet been ratified as the official journalistic voice, which meant that pompous rhetoric and uninformed blather was often the norm in newspaper prose, but there was also an allowance for adventurous and unconventional writing of a sort that has seldom been seen in daily papers since. Whatever its merits or drawbacks, the newspaper ruled daily life. It represented the most visible incursion of the public sphere into the private. No wonder, then, that twentieth-century art took such pleasure in shredding it. When Fénéon wrote his column in *Le Matin*, Picasso and Braque were just six years away from starting to cut up *Le Journal* for their collages (*Le Matin* itself first shows up in a work by Juan Gris from 1914), and the Dadaists in Zurich and Berlin a bit more than a decade from their even more violent work with scissors. Around the corner was a cavalcade of newspaper-inspired art, from the "Aeolus" chapter of Joyce's *Ulysses* to the banner-headline typefaces of Wyndham Lewis's manifestos to Gerald Murphy's sets for Cole Porter's *Within the Quota*, which featured enormous tabloid pages. Fénéon seems to stand Janus-like at the juncture between this coming modernism of machine-age simultaneity and the painstaking artisanal modernism gone by of Mallarmé and the Pointillists.

The closest literary relative to Fénéon's three-line novellas may be Charles Reznikoff's *Testimony: The United States (1885–1915), Recitative* (1965, 1968, 1978), a series, more than 500 pages long, of stories and fragments taken from court transcripts, sorted into thematic categories and broken into verse. Although Reznikoff's is a collage of sorts, open and deliberately rough-edged, with attention to the raw music of American speech, where Fénéon's is enclosed and polished, a succession of glazed miniatures, what the works have in common is a preoccupation with the cruelty of the small-time and everyday.

> Williams—a Negro—Davis, Sweeney, and Robb
> were in a saloon together. Williams was talking to Davis
> when Sweeney jerked off Williams' hat
> tearing a piece out of the brim.
> Sweeney and Williams were having words about this
> when Robb stepped up and found fault with Williams
> for wrangling with a white man.
>
> The Negro said nothing to Robb
> and was backing away
> when Robb stabbed him twice with a dirk.[16]

Both works give the impression of showing a vast succession of lit windows, a nation's worth of them, through which

---

16. *Testimony: The United States (1885–1915)*, volume I (Black Sparrow Press), 1978, p. 77.

appalling scenes can be viewed by horrified but impotent readers. Like random photographs found in a trunk, both works preserve the shadow of a great many people who may not otherwise have left surviving traces of their passage on earth. Both demonstrate that violence, misery, chicanery, and insanity exist in a continuum that spans human history; they prove that there never was a golden age.

Fénéon's three-line news items, considered as a single work, represent a crucial if hitherto overlooked milestone in the history of modernism. Even as the entries are obsessively handcrafted, the work is in a sense the first ready-made. It heralds the age of mass media, via a sensibility formed by the cadences and symmetries of classical prose; forecasts a century of statistics, while foregrounding individual quotidian detail; invites speed of consumption, while manifesting time-consuming labor of execution. It recognizes its own transience but does not concede to it. It savors the ironies of chance without fabricating a moral agency to explain them, but never shies from properly attributing the consequences of power, greed, and stupidity. Like the work of certain photographers it is dispassionate sometimes to the point of cruelty, but by the same token, respecting its readers, it does not package a facile response for them. It is a dry bundle of small slivers of occurrence that lie beneath history, but it represents the whole world, with all of its contradictions.

—*Luc Sante*

# NOVELS
# IN
# THREE LINES

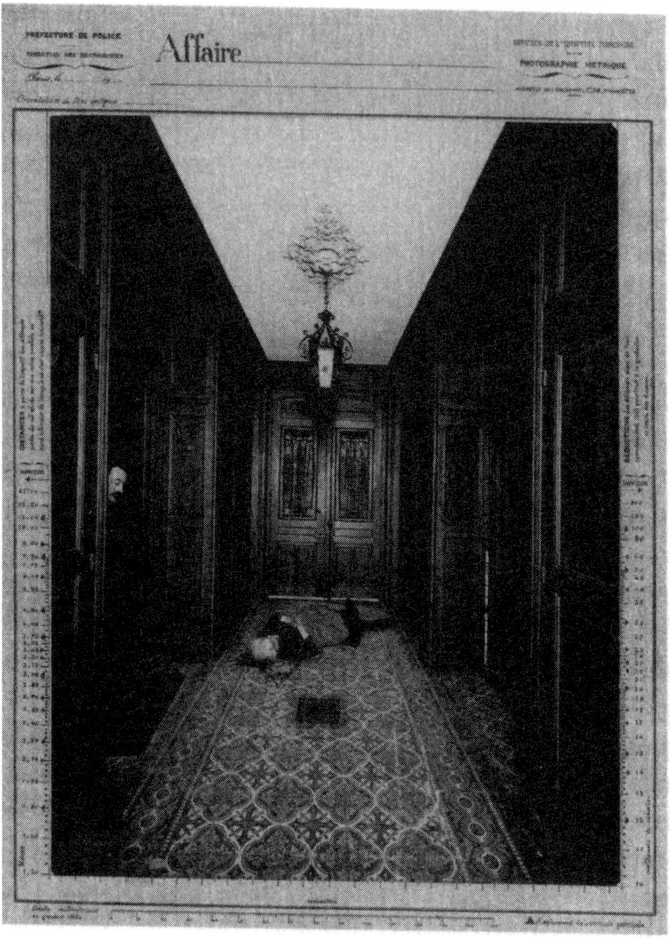
Affaire

M. Jonnart denied to the commission that the new tax plan was a scheme to make the budget's ends meet.

A criminal virago, Mlle Tulle, was sentenced by the Rouen court to 10 years' hard labor, while her lover got five.

Because of his poster opposing the strikebreakers, the students of Brest lycée hissed their teacher, M. Litalien, an aide to the mayor.

Nurse Elise Bachmann, whose day off was yesterday, put on a public display of insanity.

A complaint was sworn by the Persian physician Djaï Khan against a compatriot who had stolen from him a tiara.

A dozen hawkers who had been announcing news of a nonexistent anarchist bombing at the Madeleine have been arrested.

A certain madwoman arrested downtown falsely claimed to be nurse Elise Bachmann. The latter is perfectly sane.

On Place du Panthéon, a heated group of voters attempted to roast an effigy of M. Auffray, the losing candidate. They were dispersed.

Arrested in Saint-Germain for petty theft, Joël Guilbert drank sublimate. He was detoxified, but died yesterday of delirium tremens.

The photographer Joachim Berthoud could not get over the death of his wife. He killed himself in Fontanay-sous-Bois.

Reverend Andrieux, of Roannes, near Aurillac, whom a pitiless husband perforated Wednesday with two rifle shots, died last night.

In political disagreements, M. Bégouen, journalist, and M. Bepmale, MP, had called one another "thief" and "liar." They have reconciled.

In a café on Rue Fontaine, Vautour, Lenoir, and Atanis exchanged a few bullets regarding their wives, who were not present.

Women suckling their infants argued the workers' cause to the director of the streetcar lines in Toulon. He was unmoved.

The Yodtzes, of Bezons, were somewhat burned in a fire from which they were rescued by two cuirassiers.

Ten years' hard labor were given Tournour by the court in Nancy. The adolescent killed a traveler who employed him as guide.

No more briar pipes. Their makers, in Saint-Claude, have stopped work until they are paid better.

"If my candidate loses, I will kill myself," M. Bellavoine, of Fresquienne, Seine-Inférieure, had declared. He killed himself.

A thunderstorm interrupted the celebration in Orléans in honor of Joan of Arc and the 477th anniversary of the defeat of the English.

In the course of a heated political discussion in Propriano, Corsica, two men were killed and two wounded.

In Bône, the courts and the bar have reestablished contact with the prison, now that the typhus outbreak there has been curbed.

Clash in the street between the municipal powers of Vendres, Hérault, and the party of the opposition. Two constables were injured.

Despondent owing to the bankruptcy of one of his debtors, M. Arturo Ferretti, merchant of Bizerte, killed himself with a hunting rifle.

While thundering for the Republic, a 300-year-old cannon exploded in Chatou, but no one was hurt.

The charge of embezzlement against the management of the Toulon artillery amounts to nothing, according to the manager's inquiry.

Scheid, of Dunkirk, fired three times at his wife. Since he missed every shot, he decided to aim at his mother-in-law, and connected.

Mme Vivant, of Argenteuil, failed to reckon with the ardor of Maheu, the laundry's owner. He fished the desperate laundress from the Seine.

Finding her son, Hyacinthe, 69, hanged, Mme Ranvier, of Bussy-Saint-Georges, was so depressed she could not cut him down.

The fever, of military origin, that is raging in Rouillac, Charente, is getting worse and spreading. Preventative measures have been taken.

In the second arrondissement, 27 violations have been charged in three days against cabdrivers who demanded excessive tips up front.

Yesterday, in the streets of Paris, cars killed Mme Resche and M. P. Chaverrais and gravely wounded Mlle Fernande Tissèdre.

At Toulouse, the finale of the bailliffs' convention. Their duties, said a speaker, are "delicate, dangerous, and insufficiently compensated."

Due to their ardor during audits and polls, some congregants and a voter have been sentenced, in Cholet and Saint-Girons.

The May Day celebration in Lorient was noisy, but not a hint of violence gave the slightest cause for police intervention.

During a scuffle in Grenoble, three demonstrators were arrested by the brigade, who were hissed by the crowd.

After finding a suspect device on his doorstep, Friquet, a printer in Aubusson, filed a complaint against persons unknown.

Sand and only that was the content of two suspect packages that yesterday morning alarmed Saint-Germain-en-Laye.

The recalled mayor of Montigny, his wife, and a member of the municipal council have been sentenced to prison for strike-related offenses.

D., of the 8th Colonial Regiment, Toulon, who incited inmates to riot in the correctional barracks, has been given 60 days in jail.

A lamplighter in Versailles and a sexton in La Garenne-Colombes both found incendiary devices, their fuses snuffed.

Hanging on to the door, a traveler a tad overweight caused his carriage to topple, in Ménilmontant, and fractured his skull.

Furious that someone swiped his catch, M. Lepieux, a fisherman of Vieux-Port, Eure, nearly killed the seafood fancier.

Four horses, minus their dragoons, bolted on Quai de Javel. They knocked over a coach and its driver, Fouché.

Burning with electoral fervor, persons attending a speech by M. Lafferre in Agde got into a fight. Several were injured, one seriously.

The city council of Toulon voted in favor of an eight-hour day for the police force. Its decision was vetoed by the prefect.

The Finance Minister has recommended to tax collectors in Toulon that they be lenient with taxpayers adversely affected by strikes.

Despite a 20-year penitentiary sentence, in absentia, M. Miot, a Bordeaux architect, lived quietly in Toulon. He was arrested there.

His head injury was not serious, believed Kremer, of Pont-à-Mousson, who continued working for a few hours, then dropped dead.

On Rue Geoffroy-Marie, a young woman, Charlotte, was killed last night by another woman as yet unidentified.

Too poor to raise him, he claimed, Triquet, of Théligny, Sarthe, smothered his son, aged 1 month.

Numerous blows were exchanged in Hennebout between strikers and strikebreakers, and among their respective supporters.

There will be a students' congress in Bordeaux on May 1, 1907. The question of international equivalence of diplomas will be discussed.

Gallant Léon Courtescu, of Angers, was thrown into the Marne, where he drowned, by a husband, M. Brouard.

"Our patriotism makes no distinction between a country and the government it has chosen," said General Blancq to the 9th Corps.

In the course of a brawl in the red-light district of Tours, soldiers Machet, Braquier, and Brému and Jablot, a carpenter, were injured.

L'ASSASSINAT.

## FÉLIX FÉNÉON

In Le Brabant, Vosges, M. Amet-Chevrier, 42, and his wife, 39, are from now on the parents of 19 children.

M. Bozzoli, of Constantine, was arguing with his mother. She fell, dead of an aneurysm. Panicking, he fractured his skull.

A sort of hermit harbored by an Arab of the vicinity of Constantine robbed him of both his daughter and his purse.

Two gypsies fought over young Colomba, near Belfort. In the fray, one of them, Sloga, shot her dead.

As the matter of the Chamber of Commerce was putting the Marseilles court to sleep, counsel Aubin and the judge exchanged bitter remarks.

Mme Montet, of Bost, Loire, has been burglarized by what are believed to be relatives of her husband, the notorious patricide.

As the Paris express pulled into Marseilles, police arrested the fireman, charged with sending deadly packages through the mail.

Strikers in Ronchamp, Haute-Saône, threw in the river a worker who insisted on continuing his labor.

The physician who autopsied the mysteriously deceased Mlle Cuzin, of Marseille, concluded that the cause was suicide by strangulation.

Bonnaut, a locksmith in Montreuil, was chatting on his doorstep when the gangster called Shoe Face struck him twice with a knife.

During a pleasure outing in an ill-famed neighborhood of Toulon, Brigadier Hory, of the 3rd Colonial, was stabbed to death.

At Saint-Mihiel, A. Caillet, orderly of Lt. Morin, threw himself out the window without saying why. His injuries are severe.

Ruffet, a gunner, has escaped from the prison in Brest along with a guard. Only the latter has been caught.

Their canoe having capsized, M. Guittard and M. Sabathé, of Marmande, drowned. Upon hearing the news, M. Guittard senior dropped dead.

Through his ineptitude with fireworks, Hébré, a soldier of Saint-Priest-la-Feuille, Creuse, killed himself and injured his brother.

Fire started last night in a Bastille-Montparnasse streetcar that quickly was emptied of its riders and flooded by firemen.

M. Cocusse, in his 60s, was run over near Arnay-le-Duc, Côte-d'Or, by an automobile that was not seen again.

In Saint-Amé, Vosges, the cyclist and the pedestrian he struck both fell. She, V. Tallias, died there; he, Lacroix, was barely scratched.

Losing players F. and M. Altebo, of La Llagonne, Pyrénées-Orientales, employed cudgel and stiletto to kill M. Filian, a putative cheater.

Returning to the Labor Exchange, the Socialists of Brest complained that it was "infected by six feet of military presence."

Thanks to the munificence of the collector E. Ricard, the Longchamp Museum in Marseilles has been enriched by several works by Puget.

A car crash in Lizy-sur-Ourcq. The Combe couple were merely grazed, but the injuries of gendarmes Colliau and Fagot are serious.

Once the fire in the Deschamps bakery in Limoges had been extinguished, it was determined that the baker had been burned alive.

Weighed down with bronzes, with china, with linens, and with tapestries, two burglars were arrested, at night, in Bry-sur-Marne.

M. Abel Bonnard, of Villeneuve-Saint-Georges, who was playing billiards, put out his left eye falling on his cue.

Again and again Mme Couderc, of Saint-Ouen, was prevented from hanging herself from her window bolt. Exasperated, she fled across the fields.

Near Auxerre, Captain Morin's horse fell, nearly crushing two seated soldiers and bruising its rider.

Because of his fidgeting, police in Brest decided séances held by the bard Artigues, a candidate, were not campaign-related. Summons and fine.

Equipped with a rattail file and deceptively loaded with a quantity of fine sandstone, a tin cylinder was found on Rue de l'Ouest.

Scratching himself with a revolver with an overly sensitive trigger, M. Édouard B. removed the tip of his nose in the Vivienne precinct house.

Through a blunder, M. Vossel, an employee of the Wassy police precinct, killed with a rifle shot M. Champenois, a farmer.

It took two hours to revive Clouzard, of Sens, who had entered a gas vat to save Bouy, who in turn died of asphyxiation.

The French ditchdiggers of Florac have protested, sometimes with their knives, against the amount of Spanish
spoken on their work sites.

For betrayal of trust the adminstrative agent Vasseur, of
Boulogne, has been sentenced to six months in prison.

A hanged man, there two months, has been found in the
Estérel mountains. Fierce birds had completely disfigured
him with their beaks.

Since the church in Miélin, Haute-Saône, has been barricaded, the faithful have been climbing in through the
windows for services.

During a post-electoral discussion in Loos, Nord, a number
of persons, notably M. Contemans, were injured.

François Martinet attempted to kill his wife. He has
been sentenced by the court in Bordeaux to five years'
imprisonment.

Through negligence Launois, a servant, killed his master,
M. Paul Lebrun, of Grauves, Marne, whose rifle he was
cleaning.

After a misstep, then tumbling from one outcropping to
another, Rouge, a mason, of Serrières, Savoy, who was
picking herbs, fractured his skull.

Sueur, a smelter in Escarbotin, Somme, faces six months in jail for assaulting a noncommissioned officer of hussars on May 1.

For having thrown a few stones at the police, three pious ladies of Hérissart have been fined by the judges in Doullens.

As M. Poulbot, a teacher in Île-Saint-Denis, rang the signal to return to class, the bell dropped, nearly scalping him.

In Clichy, an elegant young man threw himself under a coach with rubber wheels, then, unscathed, under a truck, which pulverized him.

J.-C. Leloup, secretary of the Labor Exchange in Dijon, was given six days' jail time, suspended, for calling policemen huns.

Profiting from the darkness, after putting out the streetlights nearby, some people in Villefranche, Rhône, looted a warehouse.

A young woman was sitting on the ground in Choisy-le-Roi. The only identifying word that amnesia allowed her was "model."

The corpse of the sixtyish Dorlay hung from a tree in Arcueil, with a sign reading, "Too old to work."

On the subject of the Luzarches mystery, prosecutor
Dupuy deposed suspect Averlant, but she proved insane.

Turqui, a property owner in Khenchela, Constantine,
killed a friend of his wife's. She then fled; he caught her
and put her to death.

As it fell from a scaffolding simultaneous with Dury, a
mason, of Marseilles, a stone crushed his skull.

Caught in the fog off Cherbourg, the *Kaiser Wilhelm II*
made known its presence through the new system of
submarine bells.

During a small fire at the Cambronne metro station, a fireman was cut by flying glass and the stationmaster suffered burns to his eye.

On Rue des Rondeaux, Blanche Salmon twice was knifed in the side by her lover, Louis Lestelin.

Napoléon Gallieni, a stonecutter, broke his neck falling down the stairs. He may have been pushed. In any case he was taken to the morgue.

M. Colombe, of Rouen, killed himself with a bullet yesterday. His wife had shot three of them at him in March, and their divorce was imminent.

Because 20,000 francs were missing from the till, M. Th. fled Louviers, where he managed the local branch of a department store chain.

Despite the presence of gendarmes, 300 striking resin tappers in Landes continue to blockade the house of the mayor of Mimizan.

He had bet he could drink 15 absinthes in succession while eating a kilo of beef. After the ninth, Théophile Papin, of Ivry, collapsed.

Louis Lamarre had neither job nor home, but he did possess a few coins. At a grocery in Saint-Denis he bought a liter of kerosene and drank it.

With the aim of researching the effect of currents on sardines, an oceanographic expedition set out from Bordeaux aboard the *Andrée*.

The parish priest of La Compôte, Savoie, was walking through the hills alone. He lay down, naked, under a beech tree, and died of an aneurysm.

At census time, the mayor of Montirat, Tarn, nudged the figures upward. His eagerness to govern a multitude cost him his job.

A duel. A leader of decorated veterans, M. Armieux, was shot thrice in the chest by M. Pinguet, newsman of *Le Petit fanal* in Oran.

Finding that Vasselin, of Dieppe, was not responsible for the wreck of the *Georgette*, the commission decided to retain his rank of captain.

In Belfort, signalmen of the 1st Engineers, visiting from Versailles, went up in a balloon, took pictures, and sent wireless telegrams.

Strikers' wives in Hennebont have plundered the provisions that strikebreakers' wives were bringing to their husbands at the ironworks.

For pilfering on the job, seven employees of a bicycle factory in Rueil have been arrested.

A former merchant, Frédéric Desechel, of Rue d'Alésia, Paris, killed himself in the Clamart woods. The reason: stomach pains.

Fleeing Poissy and families disapproving of their love, Maurice L. and Gabrielle R., 20 and 18, arrived in Mers and killed themselves there.

Instead of 175,000 francs in the coffers deposited with the tax collector at Sousse, there was nothing.

Homesick, the Belgian Notermans, a farmhand, hanged himself in the stables of an inn in Saint-Just, near Provins.

Portebotte got 12 years in the penitentiary. In Le Havre he murdered the exuberant Nini the Goat, on whom he thought he had claims.

Sussin and Simon, of Saint-Maixent-de-Beugné, Deux-Sèvres, were asphyxiated in the pit they were digging.

With one blow of his bottle, a Toulon arsenal employee stunned the idler who had objected to his enthusiasm.

"Beware of drink and women," General Privat told the 32nd Division in his demobilization orders.

Three strikers in Fressenneville have been sentenced to jail, for one, two, or three months, according to how gravely they insulted the police.

Bernard, 25, of Essoyes, Aube, bludgeoned M. Dufert, 89, and stabbed his wife. The motive was jealousy.

Before jumping into the Seine, where he died, M. Doucrain had written in his notebook, "Forgive me, Dad. I like you."

Sixty-year-old Gallot, of Saint-Ouen, was arrested just as he was beginning to impart to some soldiers his anti-military sentiments.

Fencing master Pictori was wounded, perhaps fatally, by the thrust of an amateur, M. Breugnot.

Although none hit home, six rounds were exchanged at the Montagne du Roule between the mayor of Cherbourg and a journalist.

The sinister prowler seen by the mechanic Gicquel near Herblay train station has been identified: Jules Ménard, snail collector.

Strikers have invaded the Dion factory in Puteaux, leading the workers there astray. "Only cowards work," their banner read.

Nimble though she was at stealing jewels, Marie de Badesco was nabbed in Versailles. She got two years.

To obtain higher wages and promote their union, the asphalt spreaders of Lovagny, Haute-Savoie, have stopped work; a magistrate is negotiating.

R. Pleynet, 14, of Annonay, has bitten his father and one of his pals. Two months ago a rabid dog licked his hand.

Formerly the magistrates of Toulon enjoyed interrogating Jeanne Renée about espionage, but nowadays the subject is opium.

Widowed customs agent Ackermann, of Fort-Philippe, Nord, was to have been married today, but was found hanged over the tomb of his wife.

The unveiling of a plaque stating that Ziem was born in Beaune in 1821 set off a very un-Venetian revel, despite the painter's presence.

In Brest, due to the carelessness of a smoker, Mlle Ledru, all dressed in muslin, was burned on her thighs and her breasts.

In 20 minutes five hoses put out a fire in a loft at the Say refinery that only had time to damage two sifters.

Near midnight, M. Baillargeat, 19, the son of a butcher of Les Termes, was picked up near Porte Dauphine with a gunshot wound.

## FÉLIX FÉNÉON

Since Delorce left her, Cécile Ward had refused to take him back unless he married her. Finding this stipulation unacceptable, he stabbed her.

Strikers from the chemical plant in Cheide, Haute-Savoie, have broken windows in the homes of 17 scabs.

Sleeping in a boxcar proved fatal to M. Émile Moutin, of Marseilles. He was leaning on the door when it opened; he fell.

The adulterer M. Boinet, police commissioner of Vierzon, has been fined 1,000 francs for defaming the husband of the woman in question.

A case of revenge: near Monistrol-d'Allier, M. Blanc and M. Boudoussier were killed and mutilated by M. Plet, M. Pascal, and M. Gazanion.

There was a gas explosion at the home of Larrieux, in Bordeaux. He was injured. His mother-in-law's hair caught on fire. The ceiling caved in.

At the fair in Remiremont a lighting fixture blew up, causing the dancing couples to flee. They stampeded at the exits.

Falling into a clay pit near Longwy, Sergeant Cornet of the 162nd Regiment fatally fractured his skull.

15 mai 1895 au 151 Rue de Grenelle
assinat du nommé Balardini Benvenuto par le
Mas Louis Antoni ( Betrastie )

Having just sniffed a pinch of snuff, A. Chevrel sneezed and, falling from the hay wagon he was bringing back from Pervenchères, Orne, died.

Charles Delièvre, a consumptive potter of Choisy-le-Roi, lit two burners and died amid the flowers he had strewn on his bed.

In the vicinity of Noisy-sur-École, M. Louis Delillieau, 70, dropped dead of sunstroke. Quickly his dog Fido ate his head.

After climbing to the attic, breaking through the ceiling, and invading the premises, thieves took 800 francs from M. Gourdé, of Montainville.

Five hundred cigars and 250 flasks of wine: booty netted by burglars who visited the villa, at Le Vésinet, of the soprano Catherine Flachat.

"I could have done worse!" exultantly cried the murderer Lebret, sentenced at Rouen to hard labor for life.

Schoolboys in Vibraye, Sarthe, attempted to circumcize a child. He was rescued, although dangerously lacerated.

There were 12,000 francs in the safe of the rectory at Montmort, Marne. Burglars took it.

Just married, the Boulches of Lambézellec, Finistère, were already so drunk it was necessary to lock them up within the hour.

The *Grondin*, which along with five other submarines had been harassing battleships off the coast at Toulon, was lightly damaged.

Countering the prosecution in court at Saint-Étienne, Crozet, a.k.a. Aramis, presumed prolific thief, met all questions with silence.

Some business involving streetlights, taken the wrong way by the court at Nancy, earned a month in prison for the agitator Diller.

Marie Boulanger, a gilder, is in Cochin recovering from a knife wound given her by Juliette Duveaux. The young women were mutually envious.

A corpse floated downstream. A sailor fished it out at Boulogne. No identification; a pearl-gray suit; about 65 years old.

Thanks to General Baron Delétang, who in 1866 was interested in virtue, Hélène Dutertre, the May Queen of Meulan, received 25 louis d'or.

The transferral, organized by the Souvenir Français, of 10 hussars' caskets spurred speeches at the cemetery in Niort.

Since childhood Mlle Mélinette, 16, had harvested artificial flowers from the tombs of Saint-Denis. That's over; she's in the workhouse.

Six bulls were impaled, at Nîmes, by the Madrid matadors Machaquito and Regasterín, to the advantage of the local press.

M. Litalien, the deputy from Brest, would have toasted M. Goude. The libation, however, was a punch. A teetotaler, he abstained.

At a ball in Saint-Symphorien, Isère, Mme Chausson, her lover, his parents, and his friends knifed to death M. Chausson.

Louis Férouelle, of Louzes, Sarthe, after robbing two passersby at knifepoint, then invaded the home of two women.

A madwoman, Mme Bautiol, née Hérail, of Puéchabon, Hérault, awakened her in-laws with a truncheon.

In the toilet of a café in Puteaux, an unknown person left behind a box equipped with two fuses and filled with white powder.

M. and Mlle Mamette were canoeing down the Marne. At Bibelots-du-Diable they capsized. Assisted by M. Pauliton, the brother rescued the sister.

Notary Limard killed himself on the landing stage in Lagny. So that he would not float away if he fell in, he had anchored himself with string.

Whether by suicide, accident, or crime, Dalmasso, a carpenter of Nice, fractured his skull falling from the fourth floor.

Following the exhumation of the remains of his wife, whom he may have poisoned, M. Pinguet, of Chemault, Loiret, was locked up.

A religious ceremony and a banquet with speeches marked, in Honfleur, the centenary of Mme Rouyère.

To the sound of a bagpipe, the strikers of Hennebont closed their meeting at the union field with dancing.

A farmer of the vicinity of Meaux, Hippolyte Deshayes, married and the father of four, has hanged himself; no one knows why.

Some 30 maniacs rampaged through Bondy and Pantin. Eighteen were arrested; one had just stabbed a bystander.

Caged, tortured, and starved by their stepmother, the three little daughters of Joseph Ilou, of Brest, now rescued, are skeletal.

The hangman arrived last night in Bougie in order this morning to put to death a Berber, Igoucinem Mohammed.

A madman from the Arab village of Beni-Ramasses has deserted his family, albeit belatedly since he was tormenting them. He is being sought.

Poor man Urien was alone in the home of rich man Jacq, in Saint-Pol-de-Léon. Burglars broke in and knocked him out.

Some people were stealing cattle from a native of Khroub, Constantine. He intervened and was shot. Dead.

In Le Havre, a sailor, Scouarnec, threw himself under a locomotive. His intestines were gathered up in a cloth.

A sum of money and the title of May Queen consecrated the virtue of Misses Cours, Bernier, Alaine, in Les Lilas, St.-Cloud, Maisons-Lafitte.

Mme Sucy, of Saint-Ouen, jumped scissors in hand upon Ratier, who was exchanging blows with her husband. She very badly injured him.

When a float in the industrial parade in Saint-Denis stopped abruptly, its ornamental framework fell on police officer Duponnois.

Holding their pitchfork tines up, the Massons were heading home in Marainvillier, Meurthe-et-Moselle. Lightning killed him and nearly her.

For their dramatic escape from Roanne prison, Choullet and Chanay will do eight years' hard labor, Mettray five in solitary.

Paniosier was bitten; Ginet, also of the police, was head-butted in the stomach. They were trying to stop a brawl in Aubervilliers.

A merchant of Courbevoie, M. Alexis Jamin, who had had enough of his stomach troubles, blew his brains out.

A European resident of Tunisia was kidnapped in Medjez by two lecherous Arabs. She was able to flee, still intact but already half naked.

Their horse reared, scared by an automobile, and ejected from their carriage M. Pioger, of Louplande, Sarthe, and his maid. Killed. Injured.

Ribas was walking backward in front of the roller leveling a road in the Gard. The roller picked up speed and crushed him.

In Caen, on the esplanade along the river Orne, the students' fair (dances, wrestling matches, etc.) was jolly despite inclement weather.

Besting the French champion, who could dance no more than 14 hours, M. Guattero was, at 12:27, declared winner of the waltz marathon.

Two thousand republicans banqueted in Orléans with M. Rabier and M. Vigier. In Bordeaux, M. Biétry talked of strikebreakers.

A sick man, Jacquot, who managed a grocery in Les Maillys, Côte-d'Or, killed both his wife and himself.

With the speleologist Martel, members of the general council of Provence explored a chasm in the Var, with a view to exploiting its water.

The pleasure boat belonging to Grall, of Brest, capsized. Clinging to the keel, the men were rescued by a pilot boat.

Before a crowd of 15,000 at Nîmes, six bulls gutted seven unassuming mares, in turn were transpierced by matadors Conejito and Bombita Chico.

At the station in Mâcon, Mouroux had his legs severed by an engine. "Look at my feet on the tracks!" he cried, then fainted.

With a four-tined pitchfork, farmhand David, of Courte-maux, Loiret, killed his wife, whom he, erroneously, thought unfaithful.

Because his piety had become overly ardent, the mayor of Saint-Gervais, Gironde, was brought before the court. He was relieved of his duties.

A 16-year-old of Toulon told the police commissioner that she had killed her newborn. He immediately put her in jail.

Bracing herself on the window casement, G. Laniel, 9, of Meaux, was putting on her shoes. She rocked back and fell into the street.

Because he thought they had left him too long in the Plouescat lockup, Abgrall, a drunk from Guimilliau, Finistère, set the place on fire.

Accused of having allowed her fatherless daughter to die of starvation, Mme Inizan, a cowherd of Guiclan, Finistère, has been arrested.

In the course of a brawl among children in Gueugnon, Saône-et-Loire, Pissis nearly stabbed Fournier to death.

On account of the liberties he had taken with his girl apprentice, 13, a tailor in Toulon was arrested yesterday.

At a turner's shop in Bordeaux an electrical grinder exploded, one of its flying pieces cracking the skull of young Léchelle.

Sisowath enjoyed a private performance by some vaudeville acrobats. He bestowed, via M. Chanot, 1,200 francs upon the poor and the police.

Employees of other pottery works in Limoges have refused to replace their striking colleagues at M. Haviland's factory.

Catherine Rosello of Toulon, mother of four, got out of the way of a freight train. She was then run over by a passenger train.

While the *Hoche* was executing maneuvers off Toulon,
Clovis Guerry, a mate, hanged himself on board.

As she left a Bordeaux hotel with M. Anizan, Léontine
Cagnat was shot by the wife of that engineer.

A bomb made up of powder and 12 bullets, which failed
to go off, was found on the doorstep of M. Dubuisson, an
investor of Solesmes, Nord.

His cancer was intolerable, so M. Henrion, of Châtillon-
Laborde, Seine-et-Marne, cut his throat with a knife and
a razor.

In the course of excavations for the metro line, two sections of the walls of Lutetia have been unearthed, some
150 feet from the Seine.

In a hotel in Lille, M. H. Hallynch, of Ypres, hanged himself for reasons that, according to a letter he left, will soon
be made known.

The strike of the Oyonnax masons has ended (they gained
concessions on three counts). Those of the masons in
Agen and Grenoble have begun.

Sixty-year-old M. Bone, of Andigné, Sarthe, had, when
drunk, so badly beaten his maid that he was to be arrested.
Irked, he hanged himself.

On the road from Soissons to Melun, in Quincy-Séguy, Seine-et-Marne, telephone cables have been stolen by copper scavengers.

There was talk of a pervert, but finally Porcher, of La Grange, near Cholet, was constrained to admit his wife's murderer was himself.

A ruling by the mayor of Angers concerning parades forbids union banners, songs not of a liturgical character, and canes.

Laville, of Fournier, Ardèche, lay down, placed the rifle barrel under his chin, and pulled the trigger with a string. Dead.

A man of 30-some years committed suicide in a hotel in Mâcon. "Do not attempt to find out my name," he had written.

Typhus rages in Sidi-bel-Abbès, particularly afflicting the Moroccan harvesters, weakened by their toil.

Barely out of jail in Nîmes, Féline stabbed Julie Chalvidan, who refused his advances, as well as Paul Redoutet.

Sauvage, of the 2nd Colonial Regiment, will be taken today from Brest to Nantes. He has been accused of anti-military tendencies.

Thomas stopped the bolting horses belonging to Countess Pereira, but by that time Martel, driver of an ensnared coach, had been thrown clear.

M. O. Calestroupat met, in Parliament, a lady without airs. After a passionate night, a sodden awakening: she took him for 11,250 francs.

In the uniform of a colonial captain, the Viscount of Perruchon raked in 100,000 francs in six months. Result: jail, minus title and uniform.

A gypsy killed his wife, who was inconstant, in Maisons-Lafitte. The band decamped before the gendarmes arrived.

For the benefit of Judge Leydet, the Créteil crime was reenacted by Georges and Joseph Raoul and Mlle Grosec.

Raoul Blanchard, of the 123rd Infantry, who was riding his bicycle in Tonnay-Charente, killed himself running into a wall.

Near Saint-Chamond, an automobile manufacturer from Lyon-Montplaisir crushed the little Faure girl beneath his wheels.

In Bordeaux, Anna Sicard, 27, wounded her lover, Teychêne, in the temple and the right arm with gunshots.

Having stolen 5,000 francs from an officer at Épernay, soldier Guillaume concocted a story involving burglars, but in vain.

V. Petit, of Marizy-Sainte-Geneviève, Aisne, wanted to die happily. He drank two liters of wine and one of spirits and, in fact, died.

Sixteen francs' fine were levied on M. Godin, parish priest of Merfy, Marne, for marrying Mlle Lemaire before her father the mayor did.

Too young to be mothers, Mlle Meuzeret, of Saint-Barthélémy, Seine-et-Marne, and Mlle Garnier, of Chassagne, S.-et-L., killed their sons.

A through train passed over two 12-kilo iron wedges placed at La Taye, Eure-et-Loir, by persons unknown. The passengers were mildly shaken.

Someone slipped a mickey into Charles Boulard's drink, took the sleeping messenger's case, and cashed the checks lying therein.

Backed by a petition signed by 5,500 citizens, the Temperance Society of Rheims demanded that alcoholic beverages be more heavily taxed.

M. Alain Stéphan, of Guiclan, Finistère, although accused by his father-in-law, Goarnison, denies having set fire to the latter's home.

With a damaged tiller, the battleship *Carnot* abandoned its course to Cherbourg and returned yesterday to Brest.

A billboard redacted by the wives of political prisoners protesting the rule of Le Bouguen has been posted in Brest.

Shortly before her death, Mme Ren, of Lyon, had Mme Lefays arrested. She blamed her ailment on that midwife's practices.

At Menzeldjémil, Tunisia, Mme Chassoux, an officer's wife, would have been murdered had her corset not stopped the blade.

Fearless boys of 13 and 11, Deligne and Julien were going off "to hunt in the desert." They were brought back to Paris from Le Havre.

A virgin of Djiajelli, 13, subject to lewd advances by a 10-year-old, killed him with three thrusts of her knife.

In the heat of argument, Palambo, an Italian of Bausset, Var, was mortally wounded by his chum Genvolino.

Some people, believed to be the same ones who attempted a derailment on Tuesday, tried to set fire to the Labat house in Saint-Mars, Finistère.

Eugène Périchot, of Pailles, near Saint-Maixent, entertained at his home Mme Lemartrier. Eugène Dupuis came to fetch her. They killed him. Love.

The Snail, the Violet, and Picasse were arrested in the train station at Saint-Jean, Bordeaux. Railroad camp followers, apparently.

Supposedly to avenge his honor, Remania, a settler of Guelma, stabbed his wife five times, killing her.

Speeches and dances and a choir of 50 teenage girls inaugurated, at Neuilly, a statue of Alfred de Musset.

Mme Potereau, of Clichy, who was neurasthenic, threw herself out the window to her death. She was 30.

Because his forester's cap had flown off, Christian, riding in a wagon down a slope at Vologne, Vosges, jumped off, and, falling, was killed.

Lightning in Dunkirk struck some men who were installing lightning rods. One of them fell into the soot from 135 feet up and survived.

On Rue Championnet, Hutter, who was exchanging fire with Poittevin of the police, hit an onlooker, little Guinoseau.

Maurice Barrès, who was handing out the school prizes, tenderly harangued the little girls of the orphanage in Vésinet, Alsace.

The Civic Association in Lyons yesterday held a banquet for a few Salon painters and the police prefect.

Furiously drunk, Ballencker, of Levallois, a father of seven, shot and wounded his wife, then fractured his own skull.

With a rifle, P. Hautefeuille, 19, killed his father in Fresnes-les-Rungis, then killed himself with a revolver.

M. Deshumeurs, of La Ferté-sous-Jouarre, and M. Fontaine, of Nancy, both died by falling, the one from a truck, the other from a window.

Already there have been eight suicides in Montpont-en-Bresse in the space of a few months. This time 70-year-old Lacroix hanged himself.

An automobile belonging to M. Olier-Larouse killed old M. Montgillard, who was strolling in Charolles.

At Montceau-les-Mines, Mlle Theureau, 5, and near Chagny, M. Pierrot, 65, were run over by trains.

Because he was very poor (a wife, three children), Pellevoisin, a road mender in Melle, hanged himself.

The brutal jealousy of H. Sainremy, of Bordeaux, earned him five pistol shots from his wife. He died.

Within a week, a second case of bigamy has been recorded in Bordeaux, that of a laborer's wife who has become a foreman's.

Last night on Rue Saint-Bon, V. Choine, 15, caught a bullet in his thigh that must have been fired—but why?—from a neighboring house.

At 20, M. Julien blew his brains out in the toilet of a hotel in Fontainebleau. Love pains.

At five o'clock in the morning, M. P. Bouget was accosted
by two men on Rue Fondary. One put out his right eye, the
other his left. In Necker.

Caught up by the streetcar that had just thrown him
30 feet, herbalist Jean Désille, of Vanves, was cut in half.

Because he preferred the white flag, M. Loas, mayor of
Plouézec, tore up the tricolor, and so was dismissed from
his post.

Steps away from the horse race in Toulouse, an ex-sergeant,
G. Durbach, 31 and unemployed, killed himself.

A sentinel's shot killed inmate Chartrain, who was attempting to escape from the penal barracks in the camp
at Bordj-Choubban, Tunisia.

On a contract to transport coal to ships at Toulon, none
of the 24 bidders made an offer; they were daunted by
the stipulations.

Breaking a window, a stone put out the eye of a passenger
aboard the train from Bayonne to Toulouse. It was halted.
Nobody around.

Adding salt to the sea, the *Collburnary*, which had that
as its cargo, sank off Camaret, Finistère. The crew was
rescued.

Through a clever game of alternating resignations, the mayor and the town council of Brive have delayed the building of schools.

Did Onofrias Scarcello kill someone in Charmes, Haute-Marne, on the 5th of June? He was in any case arrested at the train station in Dijon.

The parish priest of Monceau, Côte-d'Or, has trouble saying Mass since burglars deprived him of his ritual vessels.

Because his wife had had enough of him, Noblet, a tailor of Beaulon, Ille-et-Vilaine, gravely injured her with two shots.

People harassed sexagenarian Roy, of Echillais, Charente-Inférieure, about the way he treated his servant girl, 11. So he hanged himself.

After sticking his knife six times into the neck, head, and right arm of Apolline Baron, her ex-lover Charles Selias fled.

The three members of the Esprit family, of Saulzet-le-Froid, jumped from their carriage when their horse bolted. One dead, two injured.

Ilou, the fearsome termagant of Brest, declared to the judge: "Divine justice is mine. I will go to heaven."

The city council of Brest passed a resolution urging the elimination of the July 14 military review, on the grounds that it oppresses soldiers.

"May the will of Allah be done!" cried the Berber Igoucinem yesterday, at Bougie, before the guillotine.

They're stealing children in Rouen! While someone held Mme Thomas, her mother and her sister took away her daughter.

Arming herself with a bayonet, Mme Boulanger, sentenced to jail, rushed the spectators in the court at Chambéry.

A young girl threw acid in the face of her lover, a prominent citizen of Toulon, who had taken flight after impregnating her.

In a closed session, the court at Toulon on July 6 tried the gallant Jeanne Renée who, it seems, was spying along the coast.

Someone first strangled Mme Barbero, of Saint-André-Pradel, near Marseilles, then set her clothes on fire to blur the traces.

As her train was slowing down, Mme Parlucy, of Nanterre, opened up and leaned out. A passing express cracked both her skull and the door.

As soon as his mistress, tired of his yelling, had left, H. Lheureux, of 126 Rue Saint-Martin, doused everything in kerosene and lit a match.

Two soldiers, in Nancy, were slugging each other. The intrusion of M. François Wesgerbin earned him three knife stabs. His lung is collapsed.

Algerian sailors from the *Cyclope* treated A. Bonnat, of Rochefort, very cruelly, and stabbed her lover, Royer.

Blindfolded, three Farons, ages 2, 4, and 6, were thrown into the Saône by their mother, a madwoman, who joined them.

Anna Méret, of Brest, attempted to pull her daughter, 5, from the path of a train. Struck head-on, the mother was killed, the daughter as well.

Amorous hatred caused Alice Gallois, of Vaujours, to throw acid in the face of her stepbrother, and, accidentally, a passerby. She's all of 14.

From the journalist Marodon, M. Billion du Plan, also of Bône, took an inch of iron in his side. A flesh wound.

Two drowned men retrieved at Suresnes and Le Mesnil-le-Roi. On one were found papers in the name of J. Villaume; on the other, linen marked "L."

An unknown 50-year-old, enormous and further swollen by a month in the water, has been fished out at La Frette by M. Duquesne.

Sergeant Pouget was at target practice at the camp in Souges, Gironde. His rifle exploded, injuring him. The reason: dirt in the barrel.

Drunk, P. Mérinier, of Vigneux, struck with a vine pole Cocot, who was dragging him out of a tavern. Cocot knocked him out with a hoe.

In the church at Chavannes, Savoie, lightning melted the bells and paralyzed a parishioner. A waterspout devastated the village.

Apprentice bakers Depalle, of Belmont, and Laville, of Roanne, drowned in the Loire; they lost their footing in a hole.

Joseph Vergers, of Belping, Pyrénées-Orientales, and Alphonse Jérôme, of Pouxeux, Vosges, drowned without intending to.

Two hundred resin tappers of Mimizan, Landes, are on strike. Three police brigades and 100 men of the 34th Infantry are watching them.

Bent over to add sulfate to her vines, an inhabitant of Beaune was shot in the kidneys by her brother-in-law Gauthey, who is nevertheless 60.

The stoker Calixte, who swam away, threw into the sea at Marseilles the engineer Bérenguier, who was rescued.

From the great rose window of the portal of the cathedral of Amiens, dear to Ruskin, a stone fell onto the steps.

Le Douz, a sailor, attempted to strangle Mme Favennec, 70, of Brest. When arrested he claimed to remember nothing.

At Saint-Anne beach, in Finistère, two swimmers were drowning. Another swimmer went to help. Finally M. Étienne had to rescue three people.

Incurably ill, M. Charles Bulteaux opened the veins of his wrists in the woods of Clamart and then hanged himself from an ilex tree.

Digitalis killed Couchy, a Saint-Germain woman of means, who earlier had drawn up a death letter and instructions for her funeral.

An unidentified maker of paste jewels from the third arrondissement was fishing in a boat with his wife at Mézy. She fell. He dived. Both gone.

As he was hauling up a ground line at Champigny, M. Journet of Rue Saint-Sabin, Paris, fell into the Marne. He was not seen again.

The two Crême brothers of Pantin were killed and wounded, respectively, when they stepped in for their father in a quarrel.

S. M. Sisowath, visiting Marseilles, divided his time among his dancing girls, a pedicure, and the colonial exposition.

Gégot knifed Quérénec. The two sailors from the torpedo boat "250" were in love with the same Brest woman.

At Le Mans, soldier Hervé Aurèle, of the 117th Regiment, frenetically assaulted passersby and policemen. He was caught with great difficulty.

Five unknown persons cudgeled four fishermen from Le Mans with sticks. One of these, M. A. Poiron, is seriously injured.

M. Guigne, of Chalon, while trying to rescue his children, who were rescued by others, drowned in the Saône.

An epileptic farmer's wife of Saint-Jean-les-Deux-Jumeaux, Seine-et-Marne, fell, wedging her head in a milk jug. She suffocated.

Near Brioude, a bear was smothering a child. Some peasants shot the beast and nearly lynched its exhibitor.

A jilted lover, Claude Cousin, badly injured Louise Bisset, in Créteil, as well as M. Richereau, who was trying to intercede.

Mme Eugène Manuel refused to pay twice for her husband's gravestone. The court found in her favor.

In M'sila, Constantine, Amari killed his sister, in whose house his wife, whom he had been beating, had taken refuge.

In Les Jobards, Loiret, M. David, furious because his wife loved not only him, killed her with pitchfork and rifle.

Frachet, of Lyon, who had been bitten by a pug but had apparently recovered, tried to bite his wife and died rabid.

Sweating, prostration, rash: the Picard fever. In Rouillac, Charente, out of 500 inhabitants, 150 are afflicted.

Shot, gunpowder, and nails in a bucket with a fuse: such was the device found near the dwelling of M. Martin, magistrate of Rheims.

The naval prefect at Brest has given prison sentences of 29 to 60 days to several insubordinate sailors from the *Amiral-Aube*.

In Toulon, jealous singer Rosine Ferrébeuf wounded her lover, the bandleader Cunq, with a shot in the neck.

The court at Nancy gave 15 days in jail and a fine of 200 francs to M. Gosse, parish priest of Bennay, for insulting the tax collector at his audit.

The military tribunal at Lorient acquitted frigate captain de l'Espinay, who was accused of assaulting his landlord, a justice of the peace.

A little girl who had suffered many abuses was found dead in Sallaoun, Constantine, missing an arm, a leg.

M. Ozanne, the former mayor, welcomed bailiff Vieillot of Falaise with rifle shots, one hitting its mark, after which he committed suicide.

To swindle her, Philippe, of Marseilles, arranged to be caught in flagrante with his mistress by an imposter policeman. He was arrested.

M. Chevreuil, of Cabourg, jumped off a moving streetcar, knocked into a tree, rolled under the car, and died there.

Among the Arabs of Douaouda, a couple captured an overzealous suitor and mutilated him, permanently canceling his virility.

With no attempt made to subdue it, the deadly Picard fever now also rages in Gourville and Saint-Cybardeaux, Charente.

The two-month prison term imposed upon Blanchard, of Villerupt, has been doubled by the court in Nancy, which is willfully hard on strikers.

Distinctive indicators on an unknown body brought up at the Bezons dam: a fused ankle, an infantyman tattooed on the right arm.

For equal virtue, unequal pay: the May Queen in Granges-le-Roi gets 250 francs; the one in Magny-en-Vexin, 300; the one in Argenteuil, 500.

On La Grande Jatte island a discussion between laborers Werck and Pigot was concluded by three rounds, fired by the one and taken by the other.

Fallen from a train traveling at high speed, Marie Steckel, 3, of Saint-Germain, was found playing on the gravel ballast.

Finding his daughter, 19, insufficiently austere, Jallat, watchmaker of Saint-Étienne, killed her. It is true that he has 11 children left.

A young woman of the night struck A. Renaudy a blow with an ax in a dive on Boulevard Rochechouart, then went away.

Virtue in Neuilly: Misses Fétu and Murat have been crowned May Queens. Lieutenant B., of Treil, turned in a handbag to the police.

## NOVELS IN THREE LINES

The monument to Daubigny, owed to the initiative of
Édouard Philippe and the chisel of M. Fagel, has been
inaugurated in Anvers-sur-Oise.

It is true that the mayor of Saint-Gervais, Gironde, has
been suspended, but not that he has been sent to jail.

The limbs and head of M. Louis Lévêque, of Aubenas,
were reduced to ashes by a fire. Only his torso was
found.

Scissors in hand, Marie Le Goeffic was balancing on a
swing. Falling, she stove in her chest. In Bretonneau.

On the riverbank at Saint-Cloud were found the saber
and uniform of Baudet, the soldier who disappeared the
11th. Murder, suicide, or hoax?

Employing potassium cyanide, Bel, a chemical engineer
who had family troubles, poisoned himself at 13 Rue de
Londres.

For unknown reasons, the son of a Hungarian parliamen-
tarian, M. Warmann, asphyxiated himself in a boarding-
house on Rue Saint-Guillaume.

Through chemical artifice, swindlers have been coloring
new 10-centime stamps maroon and then selling them to
suckers as rareties.

Atop the train station in Enghien a painter was electro-
cuted. His jaws could be heard clacking, then he fell on
the glass roof.

Twirling a lasso and yahooing, Kieffer, of Montreuil, committed thrice in two years, galloped away. He vanished.
He went on to hang himself.

All the riders are in a panic. The Legrand pig carousel on
Place des Fêtes in Clichy went up in flames at six o'clock.
The damage: 18,000 francs.

Thinking he recognized, yesterday, the men who assaulted
him on Monday, M. Liester, of Clichy, fired. Naturally he
hit a passerby, M. Bardet.

The fleas of his neighbor Giocolino, who was their trainer,
bothered M. Sauvin. He tried to steal their case and was
shot twice.

Attacked in his home, Rue de Meaux, by the Prunier
brothers, Terier parried. He and one of them are now in
the hospital, the other in jail.

M. Linz-Veren fractured his skull when his motorcycle, on
Avenue Philippe-Auguste, encountered M. Lardy's car.

An automobile, which quickly fled, knocked over a coach,
in Neuilly. The coachman, Charles Jacques: fractured
skull; M. Dumot: broken legs.

His wife having left him, M. Bassot, of La Garenne-Colombes, attempted asphyxiation using charcoal. He is dying at Beaujon hospital.

Nitric acid topped off with laudanum was the beverage drunk by M. Paul Malauzet, of Montrouge, when he learned that his wife was deceiving him.

In his father's garden, the colonial infantryman Alphan, on leave in Villejuif and inflamed by rum and fever, hanged himself.

A Lorraine native of 83, Mme Lautin, who had recently moved in with her daughter in Noisy-le-Sec, has been missing since Saturday morning.

F. Martineau is dying in Laënnec; he was run over by an automobile in Boulogne. In Saint-Maur, coachman Gillot cracked his skull.

A fruit vendor of Issy, Léontine Brachot, whose well is 45 feet deep, threw herself in. She was pulled out, close to death.

A merchant from Saint-Gaudens caught his wife entwined with a barber in Boussens. He fired. The lover was wounded, the beloved fled.

With a truncheon blow, an Arab woman of Teboursouk, Tunisia, killed her husband, a suspicious and brutal man.

Games of love in Béziers: Corniod, who had lived seven years with Rosalie Petit, pierced her with two shots and stabbed himself.

M. Chanudet will be confined for eight years, per the assizes in Cher. A notary in Les Bourdelins, he had, through forgery, embezzled 137,000 francs.

Dismissed by the Bridge and Highway Deptartment, Pajas, an old dock cleaner, jumped into the Garonne, in Bordeaux, a bag of stones around his neck.

The singer Luigi Ognibene wounded with two shots, in Caen, Madelon Deveaux, who was unwilling to let him monopolize her charms.

Raoul G., of Ivry, an untactful husband, came home unexpectedly and stuck his blade in his wife, who was frolicking in the arms of a friend.

At the corrida in Béziers a picador was wounded, while the bull, who had vaulted the enclosure, injured an onlooker with his horn.

After he hit her on the road, M. H. B., a Montmort merchant, put Mme B. in his automobile and deposited her, dying, at the hospital in Rheims.

Jules Rotti, one of our youngest burglars (he's 14), was arrested in Boulogne. He was attempting to force open a safe.

Because his friend refused to kill him, a 19-year-old boy of Liffol, Haute-Marne, got himself beheaded by a train.

For having refused entry to a labor inspector, the manager of the fair at Marseilles has been fined 500 francs.

Believed to be a spy, a former civilian employee of the Artillery Department was arrested in Blainville-sur-l'Eau and locked up at Épinal.

By accident or, more probably, suicide, Mme Veit and her daughter Antoinette, 9, drowned in the canal at Nancy.

What?! Children perched on his wall?! With eight rounds M. Olive, property owner in Toulon, forced them to scramble down all bloodied.

Many citizens of Dunkirk died in the war. Their monument was inaugurated yesterday under the chairmanship of Guillain and Trystam.

Nény, Pruvosts father and son, and other survivors of the Courrières disaster traveled to Herne to thank their Westphalian saviors.

In Verlinghem, Nord, Mme Ridez, 30, had her throat cut by a thief while her husband attended Mass.

Formerly deputy mayor in Saint-Étienne, the Socialist Plantevin was elected mayor by 22 votes. He succeeds M. Ledin, elected to Parliament.

In the lake at Annecy, three youths were swimming. One, Janinetti, disappeared. The others dived. They brought him up, dead.

Mme Tripier fired twice (blanks, she claimed) at her father, Marquet, of Montberthault, Côte-d'Or, in a dispute over a small boat.

Heat-struck, Hélectre, a roofer in Rheims, who was working 60 feet from the ground, destroyed himself upon it.

The murderer Bonnaud has been sentenced to death. The order stipulates that his decapitation be carried out in a public square in Marseilles.

The pipe makers of Saint-Claude, numbering about 3,000, went on strike yesterday morning over a question of wages.

A young man, who claimed to be a Criminal Investigation Squad agent, strangled and robbed, in Granges, Vosges, Miss Boulay, 85, and vanished.

The name of a man arrested in Blainville as a spy: Tourdias.
His age: 24. His profession: traveling salesman of bandages
and medicine.

Tried out in Cherbourg, the torpedo boat "352" attained
a speed of 27 and a half knots; the ministerial commission
is pleased.

In the course of gunplay among hooligans on Boulevard de
Belleville last night, two unlucky passersby were wounded.

After 77 years, the *Courrier des Ardennes*, a conservative
Catholic newspaper published in Charleville, has ceased
to appear.

The military tribunal at Châlons has sentenced Gérard to
three years in prison for matters related to his desertion,
itself subject to amnesty.

On leave in Périgueux, Pomarel, a colonial employee, out
of jealousy, wounded Mme Queyrot with one bullet and
killed himself with another.

The Fives-Lille factory will take back, without exception,
such workers (they are on strike) as will report for duty on
Thursday.

Aboard the *Néra*, at Marseilles, a Kanak groom, Vatnis,
disemboweled another Kanak groom, André.

According to the mother of little Moureau, of Maubeuge, a 16-year-old maid, Marthe Delvaux, attempted to poison the idiot child.

Despite the efforts of gendarmes, the police, and the military, a fire caused 300,000 francs in damages to a hotel in Elbeuf.

A hayloft in the barracks of the Seventh Hussars, in Niort, burned down. All but one, who is now in the hospital, the troopers escaped in time.

Two burglars were fleeing. M. Génieux, who was trying to block their path, took a bullet. Only one was caught, wounded by a policeman.

The publishers of six newspapers will be tried the 21st for allowing indecent advertisements—as well as (this is new) the advertisers.

The Rabbit of Montmartre (Lucien Undreiner) has been arrested. He is suspected of a burglary (in Asnières) and a murder (in Courbevoie).

The little daughter of constable Wegmüller, of Lescherolles, Seine-et-Marne, picked some flowers, chewed them, died of poisoning.

Vehement posters urge all citizens of Brest to a meeting to be held Saturday at the Labor Exchange.

Seventy-year-old Louis Rouquette, of Salindres, Gard, out of jealousy killed his wife with six thrusts of his knife.

General Bazaine-Hayter, who solemnly entered Clermont yesterday, enjoined his officers to practice goodwill.

The Picard fever has run its course in Charente and Charente-Inférieure. Preventative measures are cited.

Lyons carter Marius Pâris killed himself, but being a finicky husband he first wounded his wife with three shots.

Eugène Allery, the burglar who enjoyed such a long run of success, was sentenced at Versailles to 12 years' hard labor.

Sailor Renaud carried out a suicide pact with his mistress, in Toulon. Their last request: a coffin for two, or at least a double grave.

M. Husson, mayor of Nogent-sur-Marne, shot himself three times in the head with a revolver without fatal result.

The underprefect of Peronne visited villages devastated by Thursday evening's hurricane and conferred with the prefect.

## NOVELS IN THREE LINES

Fire started on the Marseilles docks in piles of copra.
From the beginning firemen had it under control.

The schoolchildren of Niort were being crowned. The
chandelier fell, and the laurels of three among them
were spotted with a little blood.

The murderers of Mme Colas, of Pont-à-Mousson,
have been sentenced to hard labor, Renard for 10 years,
Vicaire forever.

On the doorstep of the rectory in Suippes, Marne, a
harmless box nevertheless caused excitement on account
of its lit fuse and its wires.

In Marseilles, Sosio Merello, a Neapolitan, killed his wife.
She did not wish to market her endowments.

Seamstress Adolphine Julien, 35, threw acid in the face
of her runaway lover, Barthuel, a student. Two passersby
were splashed.

The pervert Charpin, of Soubille, Loiret, asphyxiated
himself and his parents. Gendarmes were on their way to
arrest him.

L'Empereur, a 70-year-old farm servant, murdered,
in Larrouquet, Lot-et-Garonne, his master, M. Dubus.

A "royal fish" weighing 330 pounds is on exhibition in Trouville for 5 cents. It has been offered to the Paris zoo, which has not responded.

A pyrotechnician of Caen, M. Lebourgeois, has been killed by a bomb of his own making. M. Matrat and five others were injured.

At Troyes: M. M.C., a hide merchant, was run over by a train. One of his legs rolled into a ditch.

The submarine *Emeraude* was launched in Cherbourg, in the presence of Admiral Besson. The *Rubis* and the *Topaze* will soon follow.

Attempts at distributing propaganda in the arsenal at Toulon by the harbor union have been hindered by new regulations.

Details of a theft of bronze (100,000 francs' worth) from the Toulon arsenal are imminent. Investigations have been fruitful.

At the Bordeaux assizes, Marthe Coulon was given 20 years in prison. She planned and executed the murder of her lover, Saint-Rémy.

At the theater in Orange, *Sappho in Desperation*, by Mme Lucie Delarue-Mardrus, rang the bell. A great success for M. Rougier as well.

## NOVELS IN THREE LINES

Someone from La Garde died, leaving 50,000 francs to the Toulouse almshouse and almost nothing to his heirs.

A brawl in Soukhouras ended with six people injured and one dead. A few hours later the victim's son killed the slayer.

A 17-year-old nanny, Camille Simon, was arrested in Saint-Mihiel for abuses resulting in the death of an infant.

News of those injured aboard the *Jules-Ferry*: Bertheaux and Godard will soon be released from Cherbourg hospital, as Boulet has been already.

Harold Bauer and Casals will give a concert today in San Sebastian. Besides that, they may fight a duel.

Having broken into the Lazard jewelry concern in Bordeaux by night, unknown persons got away with 250,000 francs' worth of stones.

In Aubusson, Paul Barraband, 24, son of the former mayor, killed Marguerite Peyrony, 22, his companion since 1900, and injured himself.

In the station at Emerainville, Seine-et-Marne, an empty train derailed, which delayed the Paris–Belfort connection for hours.

In an automobile accident at Éloyes, Vosges, M. Colombain broke his ribs and one leg in two places; his wife was also injured.

Matters of the heart. M. Simon, a café owner in Verquin, township of Béthune, married and the father of three, committed suicide.

Divisionary commander Gillet handed over the post to Brigadier Rungis and made his solemn entry into Constantine.

Mme Piet, a baker of Bercenay-en-Othe, Aube, is dying and her son Gaston, 9, is dead, their carriage having overturned.

Carpenter Agathe Borel, of Bezons, died falling off a roof, a drop of 30 feet.

Three incumbents, M. Desoyer, M. Lepron, and M. Lévêque, have been reelected mayor and deputy mayors of Saint-Germain-en-Laye.

Trains have killed Cosson, in l'Étang-la-Ville; Gaudon, near Coulommiers; and Molle, a mortgage-office employee, in Compiègne.

In Saint-Cloud, the annual horticultural fair opens today, and in Rueil a musical competition.

A Parisian singer, of Rue Saint-Antoine, M. Henry Nonnoy, 31, drowned at the cape of Champigny while bathing.

Five hundred francs have been promised by M. Delarue to whomever can locate, within the next 10 days, his son, parish priest of Châtenay.

Fire has destroyed the entire contents of the apartment inhabited by the Toupinier couple at 14 Rue de l'École Polytechnique.

Mme Céline Larue, 43, whose apartment is on the fifth floor, on Chaussée du Pont in Boulogne, fell out the window. Dead.

Mme Ernestine Gapol, 49, dwelling in Vanves, on Avenue Gambetta, committed suicide: two bullets in the head.

A streetcar in Nogent-sur-Marne knocked into a cart, the shaft of which struck a fatal blow to the carter, Baujard.

In Carrières-sous-Bois, M. Chercuitte fished out a man, his flannels monogrammed H.J., who had been in the Seine for around two weeks.

Pauline Rivera, 20, repeatedly stabbed, with a hatpin, the face of the inconstant Luthier, a dishwasher of Chatou, who had underestimated her.

Avenging her band, expelled from Cormeilles-en-Parisis, Nita Rosch, a gypsy, bit a leathery policeman from Argenteuil.

At the shooting gallery in Argenteuil, unknown nocturnal persons annexed the machinery and electrical wires that operated the scoring device.

While drawing water with a bottle in Maretz-sur-Marne, Oise, Georges Antoine, 4, lost his balance and drowned.

A septuagenerian, Mme Guillory, of Grez-sur-Loing, Seine-et-Marne, was trampled to death by the cow she was grazing.

The fall of a door knocked off its hinges by the hay cart he was driving killed, in Villegagnon, Seine-et-Marne, Bourbouze, 17.

The Lenfant Matter: The actor Iba Boye will appear today before the court of appeals in Bordeaux.

Orderly Albertine Guemon, of the 117th Regiment, drowned at the ford in Maulny, Sarthe, where the horse she was riding went in for a swim.

Saint-Jean and Saint-Symphorien hope to solve their crimes; the Marennes court has ordered autopsied Mme B. in the one, M. Vrignaud in the other.

Its grease boxes overheated, a car of the Luchon express, within sight of Athis, caught on fire. Employees noticed it in time.

An old Arab of Bugeaud, who was transporting sticks to Bône, was knocked out with a club by unknown persons and robbed.

Across from 29 Boulevard de Belleville, Sarah Rousmaer, who walked the streets by night, was knifed to death, last evening, by a man who fled.

Severely burned—her skirt caught on fire—Léonie Lefèvre, 10, of Saint-Maur, died in Trousseau.

Marie Jandeau, a pretty girl known to many citizens of Toulon, died by suffocation last night in her room, on purpose.

The cantankerous tribunal at Constantine sent away a 14-year-old faun who had, by force, made love to an antique native of Malta.

With a revolver, M. Paul Barraband, of Aubusson, killed Mlle Pérony Tuesday night or Wednesday morning, and attempted suicide.

A silent blade carried off, under the eye of his mother, the Mace child, who was fishing among the boulders at Poul-Briel, near Penmarch.

A death: M. Charlois, of 45 Rue Nollet, Paris, became suddenly dizzy and fell from the dike on which he was strolling in Arromanche.

At 80, Mme Saout, of Lambézellec, Finistère, was beginning to fear that death had forgotten her. While her daughter was out she hanged herself.

Four hundred troops of the 71st Infantry, Saint-Brieux, are struggling to contain a fire in the forest of Hunandaye.

Contrabandist sailors. Customs agents in Toulon have seized from navy ships a great deal of tobacco and many cigarettes.

In September will occur the official tryout of the *République*, which today returns to the arsenal in Brest.

In Brest, sailor Rolland, who had been heavily punished, killed himself with arsenic after having tried to do so with rat poison.

Maître Descottes, notary, fled Corbelin, Isère, leaving behind him various liabilities. He blew his brains out in Francheville, Rhône.

Its arms tied together and its back weighed down with large stones, the corpse of a 60-year-old man was found in the sand pit at Draveil.

A 3-year-old, Henri Calet, of Malakoff, fell into a basin of boiling water, and did not survive his injuries.

Lucienne Debras, 4, was playing in front of her house in Saint-Denis when the Madeleine streetcar passed and crushed her skull.

Couteau, who worked tending pigs in the woods at Levallois-Perret, punished with two shots Dreux's meddling in a dispute of his.

The madman who slaughtered Sarah Rousmaer on the sidewalk where she exercised her profession has been arrested; his name is Koenig.

Mme Thévenet, of Maisons-Alfort, knocked over her bedside lamp. Fire consumed the sheets and overtook that 96-year-old person, who succumbed.

A jury in Rennes sentenced to four years in prison M. Derrien, a notary of La Boussac as well as a gambler, who was swindling the peasants.

His sheaves were often set on fire. Pinard, of Coligny, Loiret, kept watch, armed. Pénon passed by; firebug or not, he caught the bullet.

It was a joker who put in a bottle found at Ostend a notice of the sinking of the *Espérance*, a three-master out of Dunkirk.

Auduche, who for years had been practicing theft by means of the kinship dodge, was arrested in Vincennes while playing the cousin from Colmar.

A gas explosion, which reduced the bounty of the butcher's shop to a dark sludge, burned the thighs of the butcher, Cartier of Argenteuil.

A smoker's match set fire to the heath of Kervallon, Finistère; a powder magazine nearly exploded.

The cylindrical grinders in the brickworks in Saint-Leu-d'Esserent, Oise, tore a thigh off Auguste Jacquy, 33.

The stationer Irénée Plançon of Essonnes, crazed with jealousy, wounded his wife with three shots, although not gravely. He was arrested.

Sailors fished from the Seine at Clichy the body of a man of 24, who bore a certificate in the name of Boyer.

Four guys, three who cut down hundreds of feet of telegraph cables in Courbevoie, the fourth who then fenced them, have been arrested.

The identity of a cyclist whom a streetcar crushed two days ago in Asnières has been established: M. Jules Lacour, 55, 11 Rue du Chalet.

A streetcar on the Arpajon line stove in the chest of Jules Chevallier, 3, of Bourg-la-Reine.

Doing very nicely in his hospital diapers, a 2-month-old infant has been found, in Plaine-Saint-Denis, by a piling of the Soissons bridge.

Responding to a call at night, M. Sirvent, café owner of Caissargues, Gard, opened his window; a rifle shot destroyed his face.

In a street in Roubaix, Legrand, a weaver, struck 10 times with a knife, fairly lightly, his ex-wife Angèle Duquesnoy.

M. D., a merchant of Courbevoie, caused the arrest of Dumont, ex-lover of his wife, who had attempted to sell that imprudent person's letters.

Balloquin, of Neuilly, was knocked out (with a bottle) by Tarvin, and Mme Benoist, of Saint-Denis, (with a bat) by Billou.

Give me drink! demanded Ducharie, also known as Bamboule. Turned down, he shattered with five bullets the wine flasks of a café in Corbeil.

Pajoux, who lives in Aubervilliers in a place called "Crime Corner," was arrested in the course of firing his gun at people.

Marcel Prévost fell, in Saint-Germain, under the wheels
of an automobile going three miles an hour. The young
man broke his ribs.

Prematurely jealous, J. Boulon, of Parc-Saint-Maur,
pumped a revolver shot in the thigh of his fiancée,
Germaine S.

A boar, he thought, so M. Trémollière, who was hunting in
the forest of La Lare, Bouches-du-Rhône, killed hunter
Cazalie in a thicket.

A dishwasher from Nancy, Vital Frérotte, who had just
come back from Lourdes cured forever of tuberculosis,
died Sunday by mistake.

Maître Tivollier, attorney of Grenoble, was hunting.
He tripped, his gun went off, Maître Tivollier was no
more.

Baptistine Giraud, known as "Titine" to the gallants of
Grenoble, was strangled in her bed, so authorities arrested Gnafron, a soldier.

Reservist Montalbetti, known as Gnafron, staunchly denies
having strangled Titine Giraud, the belle of Grenoble.

A rush cutter found in the pond at Sarclay the corpse, tied
up and weighed down with a stone, of Mlle Marie Grison.

Jostled by the convulsive piety of a pilgrim at Lourdes, Monsignor Turinaz injured himself on face and thigh with his monstrance.

Near Saint-Mihiel, Lieutenant Renault was found unconscious beneath a yew. He has not yet spoken and his major doesn't know what to say.

Two hundred Italian laborers (two were shot) freed one of their comrades held captive by customs agents in Homécourt, Meurthe-et-Moselle.

Urchins Fassiot and Valot, of Nangis, Seine-et-Meuse, mischievously put logs across the tracks; a freight train derailed.

With bayonets, axes, and billhooks, two bands of gypsies fought in Dombasle, Meurthe-et-Moselle. Six were wounded, of whom one fatally.

Lady passengers and M. Montgeon, a Parisian coming from Dinard, were unhurt when their automobile overturned; the driver is in sorry shape.

A dockworker of Toulon, Honoré Maffei, who had shot six times at his niece, was more than half lynched.

A lady from Nogent-sur-Seine vanished in the Pyrenees in 1905. She was found in a ravine near Luchon, identified by the ring on her finger.

An enormous flour mill, built of reinforced cement on a platform in the port of Tunis, tilted 15 feet without cracking.

Authorities hope that hunters (the countryside is dense with game) will find Reverend Delarue. The lad from the Maindron battery is innocent.

Bones have been discovered in a villa on Île Verte, near Grenoble, those—she admits it—of the clandestine offspring of Mme P.

Coachman Friant, on Rue de Rivoli, had taken aboard two cyclists. To the Bois de Boulogne! There he was shot and robbed.

Displeased, it would seem, with military subcommander Domech, Bordeaux merchant Daurat-Brun gave him a dramatic dressing-down.

Both hit, she by a streetcar, he by an automobile, Marie Chevallier, 10, of Le Mans, and Le Franc, 3, of Vannes, are dead.

Workers from the Nice manufactures of scaferlati and ninas tobaccos have been hissed at (they agreed to extra work) by the cigar rollers.

Pierre Melani, who had grievances against the police, lodged his knife in the belly of Lyons police commissioner Montial.

Three earthquake shocks, rather mild ones, woke up Constantine, yesterday, at three o'clock in the morning.

In Cozes, 150 soldiers who had marched from Rochefort on maneuver were unable to keep going. The heat. And they were colonial troops.

The new cellblock prison in Amiens has been inaugurated by young Gourson, who yesterday killed his pal Godin, 14.

Because Poulet, of the Choisy-le-Roi police, intended to arrest him, Marquet seized his saber and ran him through from cheek to cheek.

To get back together with Artémise Riso, of Les Lilas, was the wish of romantic Jean Voul. She remained inflexible. So he knifed her.

Inspired by the statue of Rouget de Lisle in Choisy-le-Roi, Marquet climbed it and made protest. His verve was unappreciated. He's in stir.

Misses Cabriet and Rivelle, of Plaine-Saint-Denis and Bagnolet, and M. Goudon of Saint-Denis, all drank: he cyanide, they laudanum.

Amiens will crown its muse on September 16. Forty beauties were vying for the role. It has gone to Marie Mahiou, a velvet weaver.

In Méréville, a hunter from Estampes, thinking he was seeing game afoot, killed a kid and with the same bullet wounded the father.

The Anti-Rabies Institute of Lyons had cured Mlle Lobrichon, but as the dog had been rabid she died all the same.

M. Odelin, vicar general of the archdiocese of Paris, broke his foot at Saint-Gervais-les-Bains, Haute-Savoie, where he is vacationing.

From the street, Delrieux threatened his brother at the window: "Come back, or there'll be a bloodbath!" He killed him with one shot.

Le Verbeau hit Marie Champion right on her breasts, but burned his eye, because acid is not a precision weapon.

Albert Vallet was hitting landowner Ferrat, of Chapet, with the butt of his rifle. A shot went off and the hunter dropped dead.

A hunting accident: M. Marie Bourdon, a farmer from Épaignes, Eure, killed his brother Étienne.

On Bécu, 28, who arrived at Beaujon hospital with a gunshot wound, they counted 28 scars. His nickname in the underworld: The Target.

Love decidedly has a hard time sitting still. Émile Contet, 25 Rue Davy, pierced with his knife his wife's breast.

Standing sentinel at night at Gondreville fort, near Toul, reservist Alison, of the 156th Regiment, fell from the ramparts, which killed him.

A scale factory was annihilated by fire in Rheims. Two firemen were injured, two children and a dragoon heat-struck.

The bones found on Île Verte in Grenoble comprised not two but four children's skeletons, minus two skulls.

A fire destroyed a furniture warehouse at the commercial port of Toulon. There were some injuries.

The salt makers of the Pesquiers plant in Hyères would like to add some flavor to their work. To this end, they are going on strike.

Strikers in Grenoble are going after cranes; on two work sites they have cut the machines' cables.

In preparation for his journey to the United States, where he will be buried, M. Stillman (car accident on July 18) was embalmed in Lisieux.

A schism has occurred in Culey, Meuse. Defying the bishop, the flock has retained Rev. Hutin as parish priest and sent packing Rev. Richard.

Mignon, an engraver, and M. Dumesnil, of M. Briand's cabinet, have come to blows in Nemours. Government injured art's elbow.

Of five mussel eaters, employees of the 2nd Artillery Company in Nice, two are dead, Armand and Geais; the others are ill.

From Grenoble last night could be seen a line of fire several miles long: the forest is burning.

Gustave Hervé was defending nine smiths from Firminy in court in Saint-Étienne. They got away with a fine and enjoyed a reprieve.

On Boulevard Carnot in Le Vésinet, an automobile drove at top speed into a flock of sheep. Three died.

Le Provost and the deaf-mute Le Tal, whose arrest in Versailles was reported, between them racked up 32 convictions and 44 years.

M. Jules Kerzerho was president of a gymnastics club, and yet he was run over trying to jump into a streetcar in Rueil.

A 65-year-old accountant, M. Leclerc, who was out of work and ate almost never, died of starvation in the Gauvin quarry.

Criminal mischief, the inquiry advised, was the cause of the fire on the heaths. Forests are now burning in Savoie and in Charente.

The coast-guard vessel *Terrible* was being given a tryout at Toulon. It slightly damaged its servomechanism.

Thirty-five gunners from Brest, who under sway of spoiled meat were oozing from all orifices, were medicated yesterday.

Some murdered women: Mme Gouriau, Mme Josserand, Mme Thiry, 24, 69, 72, of Coatméal, Saint-Maurice, Sorbey (Finistère, Loire, Meuse).

Forty Italian journalists arrived in Marseilles, where they had been invited. Hugo was quoted: "You will say: Italy! I will answer: France!"

The court in Toul has imposed a year in prison on the Andrés of Thiaucourt, who had confined and tormented their children.

Tourdias, the spy, adorned himself with an illegal red ribbon. Two months in jail—per Remiremont court—was his punishment.

It was not the meat but the heat that inflicted diarrhea upon the gunners of Brest, their medical officer determined.

Six farmers, from Argenteuil and from Sannois, who were in the habit of winning damsels at gunpoint, were arrested.

M. Dickson, of Choisy-le-Roi was wandering around on his roof. A thief! Three policemen climbed up and the sleepwalker fell off.

Dusausoy, a poacher from Ivry, who was betrayed to the police by the peddler Chérot, stuck a file in the latter's back.

The laundrymen of France welcomed, yesterday at the Gare du Nord, the illustrious laundrymen of London.

Two building stones weighed down the corpse, fished out at Saint-Ouen, of an unknown 40-year-old.

A landowner from the region of Marcols, Ardèche, only recently turned down an offer of 12,000 francs for the pines in his forest. It just burned.

Jealous over nothing, Marius Guida, a locksmith of La Seyne, killed his wife of 25 years with a billhook.

Just as the absentminded sculptor Bombarès, who should have gotten off at Champigny, leapt from the moving train, an express ran him over.

2 Juin 1898 — 119 Rue St Denis.

5324

…inai de la dame Leprince et négociante

Samson was crushed by a block of phosphate in Auber-villiers, in the chemical plant where he was employed.

Foucher, Moulet, Moerdilet, and Klepsy were caught in Saint-Denis on the roof of a house they were burglarizing.

Maxime Leroy and Arsène Méret were arrested in a café in Saint-Mandé where they were terrorizing the patrons with their weapons.

Having drunk many bottles, Léonard Vergnies, of Crépy-en-Valois, killed himself by jumping out the window.

Medical examination of a little boy found in a ditch on the outskirts of Niort showed that he had undergone more than just death.

With his forged alcohol receipts, B., from near Lyons, earned enough to keep his girlfriend in style. He was arrested for those 100,000 francs.

Angered by the harsh conditions, women of easy virtue who were cloistered and treated at the mission in Nancy have sacked the place.

A thresher seized Mme Peccavi, of Mercy-le-Haut, Meurthe-et-Moselle. The one was disassembled to free the other. Dead.

Four hundred ecclesiastics welcomed, at Moulins station, Mgr. Lobbedey, their new bishop. Five who were overcome by sacred frenzy were arrested.

Two Italian women tussled in Thil, Meurthe-et-Moselle. The husbands empathized. One killed the other and the couple skipped over the border.

A skilled boxer, engineer William Burckley, coming from Switzerland, caught the prowler Lenormand, who picked a fight with him in the Bois.

On the bowling lawn a stroke leveled M. André, 75, of Levallois. While his ball was still rolling he was no more.

At the Trianon Palace, a visitor disrobed and climbed into the imperial bed. It is disputed whether he is, as he claims, Napoleon IV.

Swimming teacher Renard, whose pupils porpoised in the Marne at Charenton, got into the water himself; he drowned.

Conaud, of the Courbevoie police, bravely halted the bolting horse of an upholsterer. He is very bruised.

Upon his return home, in the forest of Saint-Germain, Vénart found all his furniture broken to bits. The game-keeper is hated by poachers.

Grand Duke Alexis, now in Paris, was in Nancy yesterday. Since there are Russians living here, the police went everywhere he did.

The Boeuf boy, of Les Arcs, Var, who threw a rifle bullet into the firebox of a distiller, was killed by the cartridge.

At Nancy prison, Melot, sentenced to hard labor for life, doused himself with kerosene and lit a match. His burns are severe.

Facing a jump over a moated hedge at the course in Le Mans, Herbinière's horse balked and, tumbling, knocked him out with a hoof blow.

A sentinel fired at but failed to hit some people—spies, it is thought—who, he believed, were attempting to enter the Verdun arsenal.

At the Hospital for Sick Children, mason Armand Montendron, 20, was killed in a fall from a scaffold.

Accountant Auguste Bailly, of Boulogne, fractured his skull when he fell from a flying trapeze.

Standing on her doorstep, modiste Rudlot, of Malakoff, was chatting with a neighbor. With an iron bar her wild husband made her shut up.

Thrown by an automobile (license number unknown) under his hay wagon, Bouvier, of Bolbec, ducked the wheels, but he'll remember the blow.

A certain chief engineer of the 26th Artillery, of Le Mans, locked up for stealing bronze, is trying to kill himself. He is being watched.

M. D., conductor of the high-speed train, is dying at Abbeville of two pistol shots fired by his own hand.

Durécu and Cosoas have, no one knows why, knifed in Le Havre, in the street, Gaston Provost.

After he had been knocked out, Bonnafoux, of Jonquières, Vaucluse, was placed on a railroad track, where a train ran him over.

With authorities surrounding his bed, at Rochefort, Sausseau, one of those burned aboard the *Davoust*, was comforted with a military medal.

"We'll settle your hash!" was supposedly said to Guyot de Toul at election time. Was it politics, then, that drowned him in the canal?

The mountain-climber Preiswesk tottered, then recovered, then tumbled down in long leaps, his deadly fall visible from Chamonix.

Mme Jousserand, of Chambon-Feugerolles, recognized as her would-be killer the tramp Fayard, whom the cops brought before her.

In one go, Mme Matignon, of Mérignac, brought into the world three girls. All four are doing well.

Insolent soldier Aristide Catel, of the 151st, was aping the gestures of Sergeant Rochesani. The court-martial at Chaillons gave him two years!

Because he drank a flask of vitriol, Marcel Portamène, of Saint-Maur, died at the age of 3. His parents were strolling in their garden.

At Noiseau, near Corbeil, some people who remain unidentified broke three poor boxes in the church.

Attracted by his streetcar-conductor's satchel, six timid vagrants of Courbevoie assaulted M. Valtat, who caught one of them.

Three is the age of Odette Hautoy, of Roissy. Nevertheless, L. Marc, who is 30, did not consider her too young.

Amiens ran out of stamps. Bagnères-de-Bigorre finally got some, but on the other hand it faces a severe shortage of cigarettes and cigarillos.

The *Vénus* crushed against the south jetty at La Palice-Rochelle a piloting whaleboat being boarded by four men.

A beauty of Angers, Eugénie Grosbois, 25, was strangled on her hazardous bed by an unknown person.

There had never been so much squabbling at the Picco home in Gentilly. Finally the wife's paring knife put to death the husband.

On behalf of Belgian prosecutors, the arrest was made at Vagney, Vosges, of Félicie De Doncker, proficient at quelling the birthrate in Brabant.

When the pot overturned on the stove, the wax that had been melting in it burned M. Adolphe Marquet, of Courvevoie, badly.

A burnt carcass is what Mme Desméat of Alfortville resembled after she was set ablaze by a gas lamp. And yet she is still breathing.

All of the lead intended by M. Pregnart for the partridges of Alluets-le-Roi was instead taken by his friend Claret, in the rump.

A squall off the coast of Provence is playing havoc with navigation and stirring up forest fires in Collobrières and Pierrefeu.

A display of horsemen at the wedding of a wealthy native of La Fayette, Constantine. One of their gunshots killed the sister, 7, of the bride.

Imminent discharge drove Bertin of the 22nd Artillery mad in Versailles: he undressed in front of Saint Anthony and declared himself his pig.

For fun, Justin Barbier was scattering pistol shots in all directions, in Stains. Jules Courbier, a roofer, caught one.

Very drunk, Langon, of Sceaux, bumped into his wife and, because she was quarrelsome, hammered her head with a bunch of keys.

Émile Girard had a chimney fall on his head, in Saint-Maur. In Montreuil, R. Taillerot, who was digging in it, drowned in his cistern.

Born January 21, 1807, Claudine Digonnet, née Bonjour, died in Villeurbanne. Thirty grandchildren enlivened her old age.

M. Jégou du Laz, of Cleden, Finistère, fractured his thumb, index, and thigh. That was how the hunter and his rifle became acquainted.

A Nancy notary imparted 30,000 francs—an inheritance —to Reider. Some people he met in a place of amusement relieved him of it an hour later.

At Boulou, Pyrénées-Orientales, some Spanish noncoms hurled insults at a French tourist guilty of penning the graffito: Long Live Catalonia!

Witness to a medical episode during maneuvers, Mme Laffont, of Brest, insulted officer Durmelot. So he had her arrested.

Bitten by his horse, in Joinville, coachman Colignon fainted, whereupon his carriage crushed his legs.

At Châlons, cashiering and 10 years' hard labor for Désiré Lupette, who burglarized Captain Mathieu, whose orderly he was.

An angry bull was dragging cowboy Bouyoux toward Poissy by the tether. It broke. So then the bull unseated cyclist Gervet.

Rats were gnawing on the salient features of ragpicker Mauser (whose name means "ratcatcher") when his corpse was found in Saint-Ouen.

Having pulled bill-sticker Achille to the ground, they dragged him the whole length of the Alfortville bridge, then threw him over the side.

Three seals, 82 monkeys, 20 parrots, 15 cats, 32 dogs, 63 exhibitors, and their 10 conveyances were rerouted from Versailles to Saint-Cyr.

Eager for plenary indulgences, burglars emptied a shop of religious articles during the pilgrimage at Clichy-sous-Bois.

Some citizens of Boulogne half-lynched stevedore Berneux. His crime? Shouting "Down with the army!" when a work detail marched by.

After being autopsied, the unidentified bishop found yesterday on the main square in Aïn-el-Turk, Oran, was buried with ecclesiastical honors.

Zinc-smith Billiard, of Saint-Germain, father of five, hanged himself from his lamp bolt. One of his daughters came home. He was already cold.

Between Deuil and Épinay 5,500 feet of telephone wires were stolen. In Carrières-sur-Seine, M. Bresnu hanged himself with wire.

Mme Lesbos was run over by a tourist omnibus drawn by six horses. It happened in Versailles.

Stabbed and beaten unconscious, Remailli, of Meskiana, Constantine, was mutilated in a way that specified the passionate nature of the crime.

An overdose of laudanum merely gave colics to architect Godefoin, of Boulogne. So he decided to drown himself. But he was rescued.

An unknown person painted the walls of Pantin cemetery yellow; Dujardin wandered naked through Saint-Ouen-l'Aumône. Crazy people, apparently.

Bearing a suspect letter mailed from Strasbourg, Cavalier Jeannet of the 9th Dragoons, Lunéville, a possible spy, was arrested.

The Catholic youth of Pas-de-Calais will congregate today in Béthune. One hundred gendarmes will prevent its moving as a body.

Eighteen months in jail without reprieve has been imposed on Colombier, chauffeur of Robatel of Lyons, for having driven over M. Pédenne.

One false step, at dusk, on the footbridge over the Moulin channel at Dontilly, Seine-et-Marne, and Mme Louis Noury was drowned.

Silot, a valet, installed an amusing woman in his absent master's house in Neuilly, then disappeared, taking everything but her.

Reverend Cassan, parish priest of Faugères, requested release on probation. The court at Béziers refused.

The coopers' strike in the Gironde is just about over. The one of the safe makers in Bazancourt, Marne, is beginning.

Incognito and traveling by automobile, the dowager
queen of Italy left Aix-en-Provence yesterday afternoon.

Frogs, sucked up from Belgian ponds by the storm, rained
down upon the streets of the red-light district of Dunkirk.

There is no longer a God even for drunkards. Kersilie, of
Saint-Germain, who had mistaken the window for the
door, is dead.

A day of pleasant feelings in Saint-Maurice: in the A.M.
the crowning of the May Queen (Calot); in the P.M. fishing
(a contest) in the canal.

With a hook a washerwoman of Bougival fished out a parcel: a healthy newborn girl floating downstream.

The eight telephone cables of the fort of Champigny have been surreptitiously cut, a total length of more than 5,000 feet.

As jealous as a tiger, accountant Varlot, of Ivry, all but killed Mme Varlot because she had become intimate with someone.

Louis Picot, son of the permanent secretary of the Academy of Moral Sciences, etc., was all torn up from falling off his bicycle.

Pouliet and Carle were riding a tandem bike to Vanves. They were struck by an automobile whose license number they were too impaired to read.

Wearing a gray duck suit and a cap, Béthencourt, 13, set out by bicycle from Chatou to Bezons on the 20th. He has yet to arrive.

On the bridge at Charenton, the widow Guillaume and her gigolo were arguing. He beat her with a rod and stomped on her.

Several counterfeiters of 10- and 20-cent coins have been arrested in Nancy. Three were found to possess ingots and molds.

Police at Neufchâteau are seeking someone (a German, it is believed) who has been prowling around the military emplacements.

The 392 from Cherbourg to Caen halted; the engineer dislodged from the cowcatcher the corpse of Thiébault, 2, and gave it to the boy's mother.

Guichard, of Villers-sous-Preny, Meurthe-et-Moselle, was hunting as he tilled. His horses trod on his rifle. A shot went off, fatally.

At the races in Khenchela, a Berber jockey kicked jockey Rouvier, fracturing his skull, arousing the ire of burnoose-wearing sports.

Mme S., of Jaulnay, Vienne, accused her father of having ruined her three daughters. The old man became indignant.

M. Mamelle will stand in for the Minister of Agriculture on September 30 to meet the prizewinners at the fair in Angers.

A little girl, tan, plump, hair braided, clothed and shod in brown cloth, holy medals around her neck, has been fished out at Suresnes.

M. Groin, a farmer of Montesson, incurably ill, has hanged himself in his barn at the age of 39.

As a result of being hit by motorcyclist Vasseur, farmworker Louis Havart, of Nesle, has lost his memory.

On Rue Myrha, the joker Guinet was firing randomly at passersby. An unknown party stuck a stiletto in his back.

Wearing pearl-gray gloves and a black suit, M. Loubet and, clad in gray, Mme Loubet left yesterday at 6:05 from Toulon, going to Montélimar.

In a hurry to catch up with his father, Pierre Colmar, 5, of Ivry, left his mother and tried to cross the street. A streetcar ran him over.

From a thicket, at one in the morning, two shots were fired. Retired pavior J. Fouquier, 70, of Perreux, was hit in the arm and the trunk.

Some people are infatuated with telephone cables. They took 2,700 feet in Gargan and 4,500 between Épinay and Argenteuil.

With an escort of children, a dairy maid was pushing an ice-cream wagon through Avignon. The machine tipped over, crushing Germaine Pouget, 5.

The train from Verdun to Sedan came along, striking Drunaux, of Vilosnes, who was chasing his cow down the tracks.

Near Ouanne, Yonne, M. Gaston of Neverlee and Belgian
soldier Wolfgang d'Ursel have been bruised. An automobile accident.

At the train yards in Claret, east of Toulon, two locomotives
destroyed each other. No persons were injured.

Discharged Tuesday by his employer, 13-year-old Godillot,
of Bagnolet, has not dared go home. Go there, son;
they're waiting for you.

Seventy-year-old beggar Verniot, of Clichy, died of hunger.
His pallet disgorged 2,000 francs. But no one should make
generalizations.

Adrien Astier, 11, fell a dozen feet into the hearth of a
chimney he was sweeping in Choisy-le-Roi. He's at
Cochin hospital.

At the station in Clamart, metal turner Maurice Planchon
was hit by a train. He is in very sorry shape.

Destin, 20, before surrendering to the Aubervilliers
police, threw a flatiron at one of them, Lagarof, hitting
him smack in the face.

"To die like Joan of Arc!" cried Terbaud from the top of
a pyre made of his furniture. The firemen of Saint-Ouen
stifled his ambition.

Barcantier, of Le Kremlin, who had jumped in the river, tried in vain to throttle, aided by his Great Dane, the meddler who was dragging him out.

Two Malakoff blacksmiths were rivals in love. Dupuis threw his hammer at Pierrot, who in turn tore up his face with a red-hot iron.

On a gun carriage, the casket of General Rollet was taken by six mules to the station in Brest, whence it was carried to Verneuil-sur-Seine.

To thwart those boycotting the Draguignan banquet, the Socialist city council of Toulon invited M. Clemenceau.

In a tent near Aïn-Fakroun, a 6-year-old Arab girl was incinerated by lightning, by the side of her mother, who was driven mad by it.

Satagnan, grape picker, declared, "I have struck grape picker d'Ay with a 22-cent knife. Bat d'Af and Cyrano are innocent."

No one hanged the young Russian Lise Joukovsky; she hanged herself, and the Rambouillet magistrates have allowed her to be buried.

Perronnet, of Nancy, had a close call. He was coming home. Having jumped out the window, his father, Arsène, came crashing down in front of him.

At Agen, after the departure of M. Fallières, some bulls rushed the crowd. Victims: two men, 80 and 56; one girl, 9.

Mistaken for a marauder, vineyard guard Joseph Bardou, of Ustou, Ariège, caught a rifle bullet in the upper body.

The Toulouse prosecutor has launched a commission of inquiry to determine whether his strange nihilist had a good trip to Marseilles.

Digging in the dirt around a tree in the Bois de Boulogne, a dog turned up the corpse of a newborn infant boy.

A streetcar from Saint-Germain-des-Prés to Clamart struck, near midnight on Rue de Rennes, one going to Malakoff, which caught on fire. Injuries.

Fleeing the barracks at Saint-Cloud, gendarme Delhumeau committed suicide in the Belfort district.

"I'm telegraphing Ravachol!" cried Nini Colonne of Pantin. She was committed for insanity, the comrade's death being somewhat notorious.

An employee of the Ouest railway, J.-M. Legendre, 50, had his shoulder and part of his thorax crushed in the station at Mureaux.

Some drinkers in Houilles were passing around a pistol they thought was unloaded. Lagrange pulled the trigger. He did not get up.

An automobile accident in Houilles. M. J. Dubois and M. G. Bernard were injured; M. Cappiello (not Lionetto) and M. Février also, but less.

This year the vineyard workers are particularly quarrelsome. Once again one of them, at Romanée, just killed another, Cordonnier.

Mlle Clara Peyron, 65, had her throat cut in Hyères. The murderer had no other motive than covetousness.

Having come from Deux-Sèvres, hoof-and-mouth disease is flourishing in the region of Cholet, but the authorities are determined to stop it.

Too bad! Mentré of Longwy, who revealed to us he was the winner of the 250,000 francs in the tuberculosis lottery, seems to have been hoaxed.

From a scaffolding atop the Tour Saint-Jacques, some beams—the wind at 9:15 at night was blowing hard—fell into Rue de Rivoli.

The tramp Bors, all bloody, was on the road near Achères. He had been on the receiving end of his friend Bonin's truncheon.

Caught between his cart and a wall, the delivery coachman Nézé, of Argenteuil, had the flesh of his right arm torn off down to the bone.

The sole survivor of the *Coat-Coal*, Texier, relates (at Lorient) that they talked for an hour holding onto spars in the dead of night.

Capes, a landowner of Gabarret, Landes, was murdered at his home. It doesn't seem that robbery was the motive.

Woken up by the alarm in his henhouse, the fierce Dumont, of la Briche, fired. The marauders left behind a trail of blood.

The cowherd Le Maître was run over, at Le Tertre-Saint-Denis, by his forage cart, and carter Fourney, at Les Lilas, by a streetcar.

Mlle Establet, 18, of Joinville, near Blida, has punished M. Lestenaux for his prattling with two shots in the stomach.

How will we smoke? On the heels of the pipe makers of Saint-Claude, now the cigarette-paper makers of Saint-Girons have gone on strike.

Because they were counterfeiting coins, the Patry couple of Toulon are behind bars. At their home were found ingots of an expertly made alloy.

For purposes of necromancy, Arab witches of Chellala surreptitiously dug up the body of a 10-day-old child who died six months ago.

Napoléon, a peasant of Saint-Nabord, Vosges, drank a liter of alcohol; very well, but he had put in some phosphorous, hence his death.

Lit by her son, 5, a signal flare burst under the skirts of Mme Roger, of Clichy; damages were considerable.

At Bordeaux, M. Fallières summoned the engineer of the train that had brought him, and magnanimously shook his hand.

Between Paris and Arpajon, some unauthorized persons have cut down seven miles of telephone cables.

A young woman jumped into the Seine at the Saint-Cloud bridge. She expressed her regret at being rescued, and refused to give her name.

The poor boxes in the church at Le Vésinet, with its beautiful paintings by Maurice Denis, were emptied yesterday, but not by those gents.

Roger was drinking merrily on a bench in Stains. A passerby snatched his bottle, drank, and, when he grumbled, broke it over his head.

In his mother's lap, A. Meyer, 4, was killed, in Villiers-sur-Marne, by a bullet from the revolver being cleaned by Henri Martin.

Brandy, he thought. Actually, it was carbolic acid. Thus Philibert Faroux, of Noroy, Oise, outlived his spree by a mere two hours.

At Boucicaut, where he worked as a nurse, Lechat had at his disposal some mighty toxins. But he preferred to asphyxiate himself.

Watchmaker Paul S. was murdered in the Bois de Vincennes, according to the newspapers. Not at all. He had taken silver nitrate.

On the subject of the blue diamond, examining magistrate Leray, of Brest, heard from the maître d'hôtel, the chambermaid, and the barber.

Unlucky in love, gendarme Léonce-Paul Isnard hanged himself in his kitchen in the Dranguignan barracks.

With its horrible monsters and efflorescent skin diseases, a traveling freak show burned down in the park at Saint-Cloud.

Sigismond Martin, of Les Clayes, went to sleep in a field. His friends came to wake him up. They were unsuccessful; he was dead.

A young woman in a state of decomposition was fished out at Choisy-le-Roi. Diamond bands adorned her left ring finger.

Poincet, of Montgeron, fell under his scavenger's cart, his head wedging one wheel, his legs the other. He will be trepanned.

A hunter of Tessancourt constrained his wife and the other party to wait on their bed of adultery—for three hours—for a witnessing gendarme.

In the woods of Noisiel lay in two parts, under the elm from which he had hanged himself, Litzenberger, 70, his head picked clean by rooks.

Mme Fournier, M. Vouin, M. Septeuil, of Sucy, Tripleval, Septeuil, hanged themselves: neurasthenia, cancer, unemployment.

Although he got up apparently unhurt, Gédéon Aveline, of Arcueil, over whom had just passed the Pédallier's milk wagon, has died.

One of the nine children that Gros, of Bobigny, abandoned along with their mother fired five shots at him, one hitting him in the knee.

Mlle Martin and M. Rougeon will leave behind no progeny. A through train ran them over at Clamart. They were to be married soon.

Mignon, of Bagnolet, reprimanded by the inflexible Barot, his concierge, quieted him with two blows of his knife.

No one ever enters Yolande's house at Montaley, Meudon, through the window by night, so she screamed, and they took only her purse.

Madwoman Brugnet, of Asnières, pulled into the water Petit, who had held out a pole: both rescued; in Alfortville, though, Kovopodski drowned.

Since their petition for divorce was languishing and her husband was a mere 70, Mme Hennebert, of Saint-Martin-Chennetron, killed him.

M. Lister arrived in Marseilles relieved by a pickpocket of his passport as royal courier between London and Salonika.

Barnier, an old drunk of Chatelus-Saint-Marcellin, Loire, disemboweled his son Jean-Marie, father of two.

The motorcycle coming down at Mesnil-le-Roi ran right over the mastiff, but the motorcyclist, Grand, injured his head and limbs.

## NOVELS IN THREE LINES

Two horses were running through Versailles. Sergeant Michaud, of the 27th Dragoons, tried to stop them, but fractured his skull.

Trains ran over, at Les Clayes and La Briche, Buzard and Avel; love had put the latter of the two, at least, on the tracks.

Midwife Savatier, of Charenton, who might have been thought armor-plated, died of fear because a truck nearly ran her over.

Two trains collided at Bretteville-Norrey, Calvados. The resulting fire, which destroyed some cars, was put out by the rain.

Well! Neither the duke nor any representative, people observed at the funeral of Riehl, run over by the automobile of the Duke of Montpensier.

Four times in one week farm servant Marie Choland set her employer's farm on fire. Now she can burn down Montluçon prison.

The bread in Bordeaux will not be bloodied this time; the truckers' passage provoked only a minor brawl.

Stubbornly incognito and traveling by automobile, Italy's queen mother, who set out early from Dijon, attended Mass at Beaune and reached Aix.

L'ANARCHISTE.

It was believed that work would start up again today at the steelworks in Pamiers. A delusion.

M. Pierre de Condé was arrested at Craches for rape. Alcide Lenoux, who was also implicated, fled. The two fauns are 16 and 18.

The Misses Wimerlin, of Saint-Denis, are 12 and 13. Commissioner Souliard sent their father to jail because he deflowered them.

Since he holds the chair, it is by M. Mamelle that the congress of the apple industry was presided, at Laval.

Archer and Grifaut, of Nanterre, had taken 33 pounds of cables. That didn't stop the telegraph. They were arrested nevertheless.

Religious artifacts are a drug on the market. Mme Guesdon, of Caen, had a shopful. Summoned by the bailiff, she killed herself.

Joseph Bey, of Saint-André-de-Roquepertuis, Gard, has disappeared, but before that he had just about killed his brother Louis, 20.

Uncoupled from a train, a line of 32 cars sped from Cuers toward Toulon. Five of them, which derailed, are now nothing but matchsticks.

Assisted by Hoffat, Lauber beat, in Belfort, Catherine Grienenberger, who thought divorce had rid her of him.

In Avignon, former policeman Anton, who, it was believed, poisoned his bullets, fired at Commissioner Chabrié, but missed.

Although his mother turned in to the government the 800 francs he had misappropiated, second mate Martin will serve, in Brest, two years' jail.

Forty-five wanderers were arrested, the night before last, in the neighborhoods of the Champs Élysées and Place de l'Europe.

Under a series of pseudonyms, a young woman finds employment as a maid and then leaves, quickly, emburdened. Her take: 25,000 francs. No arrest yet.

Costel was drinking. Piquet, Bilon, and Nibot took off with his cab. They sold the horse, went drinking, and, in Clichy, got pinched.

Of the four shots fired by Mme Denis, of Issy-les-Moulineaux, two hit the mark. Her target: her coachman husband, who it seems cheated on her.

Authorities have released and expelled Otto Artbauer, recently arrested in Constantine for having displayed too much curiosity in Oran.

The former mayor of Cherbourg, Gosse, was in the hands of a barber when he cried out and died, although the razor had nothing to do with it.

Sixteen thousand five hundred pounds of pomegranates are rotting on the docks at Cerbère as 300 striking transporters militate in the streets.

Yesterday we announced a new rift between the metalworkers of Pamiers and their employers. This morning they reached an accord.

The dockworkers at Dunkirk have abandoned the *San Martin*. Its iron ore was burning their feet and eyes and giving them nosebleeds.

Seven hundred francs and the title of May Queen of Puteaux confirmed the virtue of waistcoat-maker Françoise Vigneron, 15 Rue des Hors-Bouts.

At the shelter in Ville-Evrard, the cobbler's shop and the poultry yard have been looted by, it is believed, former inmates.

At Saint-Saulve, Nord, M. Dutortoir, a teacher, along with his mother and sister, drowned themselves in the Escaut, quite deliberately.

At Clamart, the prefect laid the cornerstone of a school and ornamented buttonholes with violet rosettes or palms.

From the passenger liner *Algérie*, Mohammed, an Algerian shopkeeper whose business was in jeopardy, jumped into the sea.

A café singer, Victor Lépine, killed himslf in Toulouse, because singer Arlette d'Ermont no longer wanted him.

Rose, of Saint-Pierre-de-Varangeville, Seine-Inférieure, killed her mistress, Lucie Martin, with a knife. Jealousy.

Fanois saw Marguerite Blond leaving a dance in Puteaux on the arm of Pourlet. Considering himself wronged, he wounded her with a gunshot.

Some vagrants were fighting in Vanves. When the police came, all fled, including two injured, the third, Bichenon, remaining on the ground.

His foot caught in the coupling of two rails as if in a trap, Gorgeon, of Saint-Dié, struggled. A train cut him in half.

Raison, 10, was playing with a rifle belonging to Rev. Gigleux, of Tronville, Meurthe-et-Moselle. Bang! The shot shattered his legs.

Superintendent Chambord decreed that God had no place in the schools. The 11 mayors of Plabannec township, Finistère, demurred.

The Count of Bernis, secretary to the Duke of Montpensier, he of the murderous automobile, has imparted 500 francs to widow Riehl, of Nancy.

Headless, with his legs severed and his abdomen laid open: thus was found in a shaft at Denain miner Payen, an accident victim.

A party at the tavern kept by Sevin, of Garches, was broken up by a fight which, out in the street, was further complicated by gunfire.

On Rue des Poissoniers, Petit and Plançon, tired of yelling, let their guns do the talking. Plançon lies in Lariboisière hospital; Petit fled.

It's Teton who was the victim of the Montfermeil crime. Shorn of his wig he initially went unrecognized.

At all costs, the Count of Malartic wanted to hang God up in the school at Yville, Saône-et-Loire. As mayor, he was instead the one hung up.

Where to pray? Because a municipal subsidy was denied the parish priest of Martinville, M. de Verdun closed the church.

Enroute to the market at Les Halles, Achille Miltet dozed on his seat. In Montrouge he was bound and gagged, his money and horse stolen.

The little girl was coughing in bed, so Mme Ballier, of Sceaux, got up and by mistake gave her potassium oxalate in place of cough syrup.

In Nogent, Rosalie David, a poor little hash-house waitress, throttled her clandestine newborn and put his corpse in a trunk.

Near Laneuville-Nancy, at a point where the train tracks pass over a salt marsh, a hole has formed. The trains are running normally.

Mme Olympe Fraisse relates that in the woods of Bordezac, Gard, a faun subjected her 66 years to prodigious abuses.

Three bears driven down from the heights of the Pyrenees by snow have been decimating the sheep of the valley of the Lys.

The mayor of Filain, Haute-Saône, has been suspended for having, along with other fervent believers, restored the image of God to the school.

Aged 103, Mme Arnac, of Auzon, Gard, has died. Married four times, she had 16 children and nursed 24. Her eldest daughter is 80.

Married for three months, the Audouys of Nantes committed suicide with laudanum, arsenic, and a revolver.

A bull at the corrida in Nîmes (5,000 spectators in the stands) planted its horn in the groin of the banderillo Africano.

Rodin has sculpted a bas-relief in memory of Rollinat. It was inaugurated yesterday at Fresselines, Creuse, where the writer lived.

His ears cut off and his forehead laid open, Guichard was scraped off a sidewalk in Le Mans after a brawl with non-coms of the 26th Artillery.

Michel Ransch, of Nancy, cut his wife's throat and then his own. A madman.

Hoping to reach Argentina, five little boys from Le Havre hid themselves in the dinghy of a steamship. They were found at Pauillac.

No papers, just 5 francs and a gold purse marked A.W., were on the person of a gentleman a woodcutter found— by smell—hanged in Vélizy.

Hearing the boots of the gendarmes called by Rigolet, of Pecq, Drouard, his cousin and roommate, superficially stabbed himself.

Augustine Macker, 13, of Pantin, the daughter of barge dwellers, fished the little Marçon girl out alive from the Ourcq canal.

Without actually killing them, an automobile struck, on Avenue des Sablons in Neuilly, Edmond Hamon and Georges Despès.

Near Villebon, Fromond, who had been telling other poor people of his distress, suddenly threw himself into a roaring plaster kiln.

Since the Lemoine family of Asnières owed back rent, their landlord cut off the stairs. The children fell, at least nine feet.

In the Marne at Joinville was found a milk truck, its license plate torn off and its jugs empty, on the seat a corpse, that of a spaniel.

Long the butt of the jokes of his workmate Boissonnet, Canet, of Saint-Cloud, brained him with a soldering iron.

Imprudent Virginie Langlois of Argenteuil, who stoked her fire with kerosene, severely burned her face, arms, breasts.

A 40-year-old shepherd who was in love with her killed Mlle Theule, 18, of Saint-Hilaire-de-Bethmas, Gard, and committed suicide.

God in the schools of the Belfort district: the city council of Chaix has reinstated him; the mayor of Méziré has fastened him to the wall.

The pastor of Labry, Meurthe-et-Moselle, reproved a marrying couple, and the constable then had to protect him from the wedding guests.

Like so many others, Patoureau was the last survivor of the siege of Antwerp. He died at Onzain, Loire-et-Cher, aged 98 years and 8 months.

A collision at Saint-Andiol, Bouches-du-Rhône, of an automobile and a motorcycle. Engineer Mahuet, who rode the latter, died 20 minutes later.

Tartayre, of Fallières, Lot, who was arguing with his wife, killed her by throwing at her temple, like a quoit, a plate.

With a stout escort of believers, the mayor of Longechenal, Isère, restored to the school the crucifix removed by the schoolmaster.

Nothing remains in the poor boxes or on the altars of the churches of Bezancourt and Boult, Marne; burglars came by.

The delegates of the International Commercial Association of London were greeted warmly in Lyons. There were banquets, speeches, toasts.

With club and rifle butt—all because he was jealous—Jourdain, of Mézières, Sarthe, beat Letourneau.

## FÉLIX FÉNÉON

In Saint-Cyr, Georges Mahler was fencing with his knife against a lamppost. All he managed to do was cut the artery in his right wrist.

Almost 70 and utterly ruined, M. Vincent, a former merchant, cut his throat with a kitchen knife, in Clichy.

The Italian artists' model Giuseppe Ferrero, who lived in Chaville in a house in ruins, has been arrested for his political opinions.

Catching burglars in the act, M. Duvignier, a geometrician of Sceaux, took down his carbine. He was bound and gagged and his safe was forced.

Two quarrymen of Vaucouleurs were caught in an avalanche of sand. Pépin was pulled out safely but Paxel died.

What were those two persons doing at night on the embankment of the Apollinaire redoubt? Two soldiers fired. They missed.

On account of his zeal at keeping Jesus in the schools, M. de Blois was relieved of his duties as mayor of Coat-Méal.

The bridge at El Kantara stands 270 feet above the ravine. Cross, 16, of Constantine, made the leap. Her father thwarted her love.

When M. Mével, pastor of Saint-Eutrope in Morlaix,
and his maid came home, the maintenance-fund cashbox,
1,224 francs and 65 cents, was gone.

Frédéric Pénaut, of Marseilles, has a wife and a brother.
The two were in love. Or so he believed, and he wounded
his rival with two shots.

Couderc, of the 129th Regiment at Le Havre, requested
discharge on account of deafness. In vain. So he committed
suicide.

Louis Gaux, 21, of Levallois-Perret, was knifed by a young
woman wandering about by night in the military zone.

Either for sport or to cause a fire someone, at night, in
Bonnières, shot up a gaslight next to a kerosene tank.

In four years M. Renard, of Verrières, would have turned
80. But he suffered too much from his heart ailment. He
committed suicide.

A bottle floated by. Mauritz, of Sèvres, leaned over to grab
it and fell into the Seine. He is now in the morgue.

Two Great Danes drove away people who, intending theft,
entered the home at Rochefort of Mlle Louise Clemenceau,
a relative of the minister.

Harassed by parental lectures, Mlle Rosalie Blénard, 17, of Saint-Denis, threw herself out the window. She broke her legs.

Alexandre Daubat, 48, a quarryman of Villejuif, could not get over his wife's leaving him. He hanged himself in his orchard.

It was impossible to break into the safe belonging to horticulturist Poitevin, of Clamart. Vexed, the burglars set his barn on fire.

Struck by a motorcycle on the bridge at Charenton, Roblot, a cooper, executed a 12-foot leap, but landed on the roadway.

Between Ville-du-Bois and Montlhéry, vagrants beat to a pulp Thomas, a tailor, and emptied his pockets.

The marquis of Trévaudans, a farmworker in Sonchamps, ably exonerated himself of suspicions that he had robbed his friend Coiscien.

The hog dealer Dauvilliers was seriously injured when M. G. Barry's automobile blindsided his cart in Versailles.

A well-known prosecutor, M. Germain, is on the trail of Hermann Schirschini, a.k.a. Ezarefs, guilty of many murders in Switzerland.

With her dress over her head because it was raining hard, Mme Rossy, of Levallois, failed to hear the electric car that ran her over.

A young brunette in a black tailored suit, whose delicate undergarments were monogrammed M.B.F., was fished out at Saint-Cloud bridge.

Forty gypsies, along with their camels and bears, were forced by gendarmes to leave Fontenay-aux-Roses and for that matter the Seine.

At the Levallois city council, matters invariably stand at 17 for, 17 against. The dissolution of that body appears inevitable and imminent.

Twelve votaries of the order of Jean-Baptiste de la Salle have been living in a clandestine community at Marseilles. They have been warned.

Arrested in Aubervilliers was Briancourt, 17. Recently, in Saint-Denis, he killed Dequinquier, but in self-defense, he insisted.

An unidentified cyclist knocked over, at night in Fourqueux, wheelwright Garnier, 58, who sustained severe injuries to the head.

Martin, a fairly mysterious character, with a star tattooed on his forehead, was fished out at the dam in Meulan.

Collision in Suresnes, automobiles of M. Alain and Émile Pathé. Bruised here and there, M. Pathé was brought home to 98 Rue de Richelieu, Paris.

As if in mythological times, a ram has assaulted a shepherdess of Saint-Laurent, in the bed of the Var, where she was grazing her flock.

Calling himself the Count of Saint-Hilaire, a soldier of the 24th Colonial Regiment was swindling women in Perpignan. He was arrested.

At Villerupt, in a brawl between French and Italian workers, one of the latter, Cola, accidentally killed his compatriot Biancani.

For having put God back in schools or having prevented his being removed, the mayors of Coquerel and Fricourt, Somme, have been ousted.

The pilot boat *Reine-d'Arvor* has capsized off Molène island. There are two victims: Créach and Couillandre.

At Cannes was held the wedding of Jean-Georges de Saxe and Marie-Immaculée de Bourbon-Siciles. The king of Saxony was present.

Mme Guibert herself, 82, grappled with H. Jouve, the pervert. She pressed charges. M. Germain, judge of Estampes, has ordered an inquiry.

The Englishman James, a suburban celebrity (athletic feats, rowing), cut his throat at Courbevoie; he feared becoming insane.

On Rue Lecuyer in Aubervilliers, at different times in a single day, were found two injured persons (Huques and Savary) and one dead (Ramin).

In a feverish delirium, Mme Tobeau, 36, jumped out her window on Rue Magenta in Coubevoie. The leap was fatal.

Mme Gillot of Drancy died in her cistern. She was drawing water and leaned over too far.

Some 70-year-olds killed themselves: Edouard Lequent, of Île-Saint-Denis (rope); peddler Bouillon, in the Meudon woods (revolver).

Unemployed Périer tried to asphyxiate himself in Garches, along with his son, 9, who was starving. He was charged with attempted homicide.

"Let me die quietly; I won't say anything," said Devinder, 19, knifed at five in the morning on Place Carnot in Saint-Denis, to the police.

They're leaving, those Laotian dancers who graced the fair at Marseilles; they're leaving today aboard the *Polynésien*.

A complaint from the Ministry of War was sent yesterday to the prosecutor in Marseilles, its subject M. Vignaud, of *La Voix du peuple*.

In the tunnel at Baume-les-Dames, Doubs, a freight train derailed. The engineer broke two of his teeth.

The mayor of Chaux, Belfort district, has been dismissed; he wished at all costs to hang the effigy of God in the sight of schoolchildren.

Once again Christ is on the walls of the schools of Ruaux, Vosges, the work of the mayor, Paul Zeller, who is one of the zealots.

Count Gurowsky de Wezele has donated to the Arbitration Society his château at Mount Boron; it will become a "museum of peace."

At night, in Bezons, Charrault awakened his three brothers-in-law from their conjugal beds by firing at their windows.

Once again, people have been stealing telephone cables: in Paray, Athis-Mons, and Morangis, 36,600 feet; in Longjumeau, 10 miles.

In the military zone, at two in the morning, the actor Michel Trubert was hit with a club and his clothing was stolen.

Their secularization having proved false, a summons was given to three Ursuline nuns who were teaching in a school in Auxerre.

Because an automobile ran over his dog, a peasant from Dardilly, Rhône, shot at another automobile. He got a year in jail, suspended.

The Toulouse sportsman Pierre de Carayon-Talpayrac, 43, was arrested for burglary and arson.

In the morning, Kerligant was released from prison in Versailles; that night he was back, having provoked the irritability of a gendarme.

Stunned by a blow with brass knuckles and then gagged, market gardener Lody, of Vaucresson, was robbed on the road at dusk.

The prefects of Maine-et-Loire and Marne have inflicted the martyrdom of suspension upon four mayors who wanted God in the schools.

Donatien Renaud, of Esnandes, Charente-Inférieure, died of his burns in the municipal lockup, which he drunkenly set on fire.

At Genon, on the outskirts of Bordeaux, Buile was killed and Gazare wounded by Spaniards who immediately fled the country.

Weaver F. Pérout, of Golbey, Vosges, was shot in the groin by his foreman, Gaspard, whom he was threatening.

Bartani, of Béziers, a widow because she had killed her husband, ripped up Roffini's nose with a pistol shot. "A man? A dog!" said she.

There have been five arrests at Montbrison (three in the barracks, two in town) over eight shoes stolen from a regimental store.

Three drunks of Lyons were hitting Mlle Anselmet, a café manager. Her lover intervened, shooting, killing one and wounding her.

"Fine. I won't bother you any longer!" said M. Sormet of Vincennes to his wife and her lover, and blew his brains out.

Young Jault broke his nasal septum, tore off his lips, and cut his tongue in falling from his bicycle at Saint-Jean-les-Deux-Jumeaux.

The Authors League demanded royalties from the pastor of Vaux-sur-Seine for a religious concert. He refused. The prefect will issue a writ.

In the gravel pit at Rueil, Paul Roblin, 10, of Nanterre, split open his forehead on a rail while scavenging for coke.

Jewelry broker Brucknoff, of Prague, allowed his precious satchel to be stolen, at night, on the Chemin des Tybilles, near Suresnes.

An irascible conversationalist, Convest, of Thiais, struck with an iron bar the head of his interlocutor, Milot, of Choisy-le-Roi.

For 11 days three shipwrecked sailors from the *Georges-René* drifted in a dory. A three-master picked them up; they are now in La Rochelle.

Choosing solidarity with God in the matter of the schools, factory owner Henry, of Brévilly, Ardennes, resigned his post as mayor.

Citizens and gendarmes of Tonnay-Charente were chasing the old prowler Raud through the marshes. He wounded one and was riddled with bullets.

Near Gonesse, Louise Ringeval, 4, fell from a through train, was picked up by an express, was returned to 16 Rue Daval, Paris, barely scratched.

It was unlucky of Renaud to have ventured within rifle range of Professor Thalamas, who was hunting in Gambais. He is at death's door.

104 (a name worn by the wrestler Nassé) dallied with a delicate actress in Versailles. The real Mme 104 chastised him, with a knife.

Nothing but plate! At least the finger of Saint Louis had to be authentic, so the people who robbed the church at Poissy took it.

Their automobile skidded and threw into a pond, at Sartoire, four salesmen. Another automobile, in Boissy-le-Sec, ran over M. Chanteloup.

The 110 shuttle derailed at the switch in Chars. No one was hurt, but there were delays for six hours.

Her daughter dead, her son far away, Mme Boulet, of Le Buchet, township of Buhy, hanged herself out of hopelessness.

Taking advantage of the dark, bandits attempted to board the automobile belonging to ship's captain Goydet, between Toulon and Tamaris.

At Yzeure, Allier, where the croup is raging, often fatally, the schools have been shut and will be disinfected.

Medical treatment is being given, at Mantes, to motorcyclist Pierre Devine, 26, who skidded at Flins and broke his right arm.

A young woman, Mlle Pradat, committed suicide by jumping out the window of the apartment she shared with her mother, in Neuilly.

In a lime kiln on Avenue Pierrefitte in Villetaneuse, the old tramp Méry was found asphyxiated.

Mme Bardin and M. Blais are in the hospital at Saint-Maurice. They didn't hear an eastbound Parisian coming, and were hit.

On the stake where they tied him up, four amateur policemen beat with sticks the young thief Dutoit, of Malakoff, whom they caught.

The car (driver: Touldoire) that had just hit him at La Patte-d'Oie-d'Herblay brought Lenugue back to his home.

Chased by a naval gendarme, a sailor dove into a pile of sheet-metal scraps, one of which severed his carotid artery.

Because one of their number was dismissed and a delegation was refused audience by the manager, 100 streetcar workers of Nancy are on strike.

After three days and two nights of deliberations, the jury at Foix acquitted both cousin and shepherd of the murder of Rouzaud at Montaillon.

The Nancy prosecutor arrested two young girls, has threatened others, looks out for obliging matrons; he wants some real action.

Maître Noury, notary of Fougères, indicted for embezzlement and forgery, has fled, pursued by a warrant for his arrest.

One more item in the martyrology of those mayors who consider the deity indispensible in school: the one at Bourg-Blanc has been dismissed.

A fire, damages of which are estimated to be 40,000 francs, has destroyed the warehouse of a brewer, Hanus, of Saint-Dié.

Three miles upstream from Nice, the river Paillon has overflowed its banks due to rain, taking with it the street-car line under construction.

Tenant farmer Nicol, of Montréal, Aude, moved away, leaving his mother, 77, in the pigsty. The farm manager found her there, dying.

Suicide: A 60-year-old woman, Mme Navette, of Cluny, blind for five years, doused herself with mineral oil and lit a match.

Fire started in the very center of Lannemezan, Haute-Garonne, and ravaged or destroyed the town hall and eight houses.

Eight young Spaniards have been found dead less than a mile from the shelter at Rioumajou, in the Pyrenees; snow overtook them October 31.

M. Thalamas has been hunting furiously in Gambais, but he hasn't hurt anyone; only the game is imperiled by his excellent rifle.

A feebleminded woman, B. Nourry, ragpicker in Arcueil and prey to the little neighborhood rascals, has died either of fear or of her wounds.

In vain, the examining magistrate of Meaux questioned him for two hours, but Maitrugue, who is suspected of espionage, remained impenetrable.

In the freight cars that brought the three victims of the *Lutin* to Brest, their families sat on chairs and cried and prayed all night.

On Avenue de la Motte-Piquet, firemen were called in to unblock the wheels of the streetcar that had run over an unknown woman.

While having words with Jeannot, a gardener of Ivry, gardener Buisson, of Paris, was hit on the head with a spade.

Unhorsed near Versailles, M. Blanchon, commander of the 22nd Artillery Regiment, remained on the ground in a faint.

Still no news of Voiry, the clerk who vanished October 16 with 1,000 francs, retrieved. He is being sought in the thickets of Saint-Germain.

In a dive in Versailles, the ex-priest Rouslot obtained with his eleventh absinthe the attack of delirium tremens that did him in.

On the bridge at Saint-Cyr, painter Maurice awaited his girlfriend. She was late. He shot and killed himself: drunkenness and neurasthenia.

Curtet is dying in a hospital in Versailles, hit on the head with a pan by the chestnut vendor Vaissette.

Émilienne Moreau, of Plaine-Saint-Denis, had thrown herself in the drink. Then she leaped four floors. Still alive, but she'll reconsider.

The waiter Vastaud, of Sèvres, was already lying on the ground gagged when with two pistol shots he sent his attackers flying.

In the throes of fever, Jules Robin, of Villejuif, jumped out the window. He lived on the fifth floor.

Rather than paying him for the alcohol they were full of, three drinkers beat up Drich. Citizens of Villetaneuse nearly lynched them.

In Rueil, the interurban hit Doby. Police and firemen rushed to the scene. But there was nothing left; it had carried away its victim.

The ferryboat *La Seyne-Toulon* was hit hard either by the *Cigogne* or by the *Alose*, respectively a submersible and a submarine, on dives.

To ensure his place in heaven, Desjeunes of Plainfang, Vosges, had covered with holy pictures the bed where he killed himself with rum.

After an absence of eight days, Master Sergeant Retz returned to the 18th Artillery Regiment yesterday and shot himself in the heart.

Moliterni tried to kill Abril, of Marseilles, at whose house he was keeping his mistress, Bisio. For him: death; for her: 20 years.

Somebody (Bouteiller) was, at night, molesting Davranches's cows, at Haucourt, Seine-Inférieure. Davranches, on lookout, killed him.

Not without difficulty, the gendarmes of Puget-Théniers managed to escape their barracks, surrounded by the overflowing Var river.

V. Kaiser, 14, was headed to Mont-Saint-Martin, Meurthe-et-Moselle, to see her father. Then the satyr of the woods rose up before her...

Near Couhé, Vienne, M. Blanc's automobile knocked over a bicycle; the cyclist, M. Leblanc, was picked up in a lamentable state.

Delalande's tender feelings for his maid were such that he killed his wife with a pitchfork. The Rennes assizes sentenced him to death.

M. Usuello and M. Crespi were very cold (30° below) at 18,000 feet aboard the *Milano*, taking off from Milan and landing at Aix-en-Savoie.

Colics are tormenting 18 inhabitants of Matha, Charente-Inférieure; they ate some mushrooms that were much too lovely.

Pharmacist and Republican, M. Estève was elected to the general council at Sournia, Pyrénées-Orientales, beating Rives, physician and Socialist.

A suicide and an accident: trains ran over shepherd Pichon, of Simandre, Ain, and a road mender at Famechon, Somme.

In a ditch at Vis-à-Marles, Pas-de-Calais, day laborer Jean-Baptiste Despret, 59, lay, knocked unconscious.

Albert Cauvin was arrested at Saint-Lazare station. He is supected of forgery and swindles. A search of his six trunks proved fruitful.

The rusted revolver fired by Demons, 15 Rue de l'Ouest, exploded, tearing off his hand and riddling his body with steel.

Crossing the tracks at the Orléans station, Germain Delbas caught his foot in the fork of two rails. A passing train crushed his arm.

The rope of the winch that was loading bags of oats aboard the Russian steamer *Rockeliv* strangled Rochefort stevedore Honoré Geoffroy.

The tramp Vernier is suspected of being the killer of Étienne Roblot, a laborer of Montmaçon, Côte-d'Or.

The 515 ran over Mme Dutertre at the grade crossing in Monthéard, Sarthe. An accident, it is believed, although she was very poor.

More than a mile of telephone cable was cut between Arcueil and Bourg-la-Reine and two and a half in Pavillons-sous-Bois.

Foringer, alias Rothschild, a Pantin ragpicker, came home drunk, drained a liter of wine despite his son's protests, and broke it over his head.

Burglars' wagons hauled away furniture, bronzes, and wines from the villas in Clamart of M. Pigelet, M. Baguet, and M. Verdier.

While pretending to search through her hoard for rare coins, two con women took 1,800 francs' worth of common ones from a lady in Malakoff.

Although it had arrived at the station in Vélizy, the train was still rolling. The impatient Mme Gieger broke both her legs.

Persons unknown have collected the contents of the poor boxes in the churches of Saint-Germain-lès-Arpajon and Bruyères-le-Châtel.

A poor boy of about 15 jumped into the canal at Plaine-Saint-Denis. They extended a pole, but he pushed it away and sank like a stone.

On the left shoulder of a newborn, whose corpse was found near the 22nd Artillery barracks, a tattoo: a cannon.

Too many people threaten, "I'll cut off your ears!" Vasson, of Issy, made no such pronouncement to Biluet, but cropped him nevertheless.

Four more mayors have been suspended in Maine-et-Loire. They wanted to keep the spectacle of the death of God in the sight of schoolchildren.

Love. In Mirecourt, the weaver Colas lodged a bullet in the brain of Mlle Fleckenger, and treated himself with equal severity.

Behind the casket, Mangin, of Verdun, was making his way. He did not reach the cemetery that day, however. Death overtook him enroute.

Cantrelle and Grenet were fishing off the coast of Fécamp. Their dory capsized. The sea has yet to give up more than one corpse.

Lunarès, his wife, and Roca the barber, who blackmailed the clients of midwives, have been pinched in Rouen.

On Rue de Flandre, Marcel Baurot, whose quintuple amputation proved fatal, cut off his fingers with an electric saw.

Thibault and Banicot were forcing open a safe on Rue Cugnot. Disturbed, they started shooting, and the noise led to their arrest.

When the midnight streetcar, supposed to take them to Pierrefitte, went out of order, 30 passengers waited for hours at Saint-Cloud.

# FÉLIX FÉNÉON

When drunk, plumber Laplant, of Meudon, became affable. His companions knocked him out with brass knuckles and robbed him.

On Rue Poliveau and Rue Lacépède, Louis Bériard and Édouard Dessain attempted suicide, the latter for the third time.

M. Cauvin, who was arrested the day before yesterday, was let go. The plaintiffs exaggerated. He was simply ingenious at procuring money.

Two mayors in the Somme were determined to restore to classroom walls the image of divine torture. The prefect suspended those mayors.

It took at least half an hour to retrieve Inghels from the pile of logs that had fallen on him, Quai d'Austerlitz.

When Bellanger, of Prunay-sous-Ablis, was found throttled and hanged, his son-in-law, Faudoire, was arrested. He furnished an alibi.

The gendarmes of Morlaix were sent to Plougar to substitute lay teachers for the nuns who had barricaded themselves in the school.

Mlle Jeanne Guillaume, of Rue de Buci, opened the veins of her arms in the bath.

Tailor Marck was 60 years old. There is no work available for someone that old. He and Héloïse Roncier asphyxiated themselves.

Alfred Leroux, 22, of Lens, coveted Mlle Mathilde Huleux, 23, of Pont-à-Vendin. She resisted him; he murdered her.

A fight in Remiremont between night watchman Duchiez and three men who were looting a draper's wagon, and whom he did not succeed in catching.

In the evening, Blandine Guérin, of Vaucé, Sarthe, undressed on the stairs and, bare as a schoolhouse wall, drowned herself in the well.

It has proved impossible to find, aboard the *Amiral-Aube*, certain pieces of the telephone-loudspeaker equipment in the blockhouse.

Stoker's mate Jules Pietri, of the *Algésiras* at Toulon, got himself caught in machinery, which mutilated him.

Versailles tavern keeper Maurice Berger has been arrested; for two years he had been keeping prisoner Victorine Brazier, a woman of 65.

Xavier Dubreuil, employee of a spinning mill, detrained at Charmes, hometown of M. Barrès. A train coming the other way pulverized him.

At dawn, Mlle Eugénie Gilbert, of Redon, to whom love had been cruel, went off to throw herself into the Nantes Canal at Brest.

A dark, rainy night. The cart driven by Bomer, of Changé, Sarthe, was hit on the road by a streetcar. Bomer in very bad shape.

Attempting to escape from an insane asylum, Madec injured an attendant and killed an inmate. The Rouen assizes gave him 12 years' prison.

In their carriage, at night, on the road from Sedan to Remilly, butcher Parpaite killed his wife. He had originally mentioned suicide.

Oranges, 572,000 pounds' worth, are sitting on the docks at Cerbère waiting for transport workers and stevedores to come to terms.

Taken for 15,550 francs by Louise Lepetit, the Turkish merchant Soleiman had her arrested; reimbursed by Fat Jules, he dropped the charge.

Louis Tiratoïvsky mortally wounded, in Aubervilliers, Madame Brécourt, and committed suicide. Love.

Jules Marty, 56, a mercer's clerk, and his wife, 38, asphyxiated themselves in Saint-Ouen. Poverty.

From a scaffold a heap of tiles fell on the head of Sosthène Lerizou, a glover of Le Perreux.

The Pouvret and Vivier villas, at Bellevue and Val-Fleury, have been looted and even stripped of their lead pipes.

In order to see the world, Louis Legrand, Bedroux, and Lenoël, with a collective 36 years to go, escaped from the penal colony at Gaillon.

Swindler of the shareholders of his insurance company (life, accident, fire), M. Gérodias was arrested in Enghien.

Lasson, of Courcelles-sous-Jouarre, was hit by a train; Escoffre, of Cabaniel, Haute Garonne, assaulted; Bailly, of Remiremont, asphyxiated.

Albert has drawn a 600 franc fine; in the Coupe des Pyrenées he drove his car with a daring that proved fatal to M. Salvaire, of Limoux.

Jubert, day laborer of Le Mans, admits that he often substituted for his wife his daughter Valentine, 14, who was 8 when the practice began.

Calen, an inmate at Thouars prison, who had just been missed in the head count, was killed falling from a crag. He was trying to escape.

Arthur Arnould had already collected three sets of hand bells from churches and bells from 27 bawdy houses when he was arrested.

At the cemetery in Essarts-le-Roi, M. Gauthier had buried his three daughters. He wanted to have them exhumed. One corpse was missing.

When he came home, Vauthier, a worker of La Chapelle-au-Bois, Vosges, found his wife drunk, and virtuously throttled her.

Seminarian Rivollier, of Saint-Bonnet-de-Joux, Saône-et-Loire, received a waybill. His emotion was such that he fell unconscious and died.

A. Tharaud, who killed with his automobile Geneviève Jourdain, 8, was sentenced at Le Havre to two months' prison and 6,600 francs in damages.

In sight of the druggist who was her lover, a young woman of Toulouse killed herself with a shot to the heart.

Suicide. At Toul, soldier Henrion, of the 26th Artillery Regiment, pierced his heart with a shooting-gallery bullet.

"It's pestilential!" exclaimed the Undersecretary of War as he left the barracks in Brest of the 2nd Colonial Regiment.

Fontanières stabbed Casterès. Replete with the favors of Mlle Lacombe, like so many citizens of Toulouse, they were mutually jealous.

In his seat in the truck, Parisian mover Jean Gervat dozed. He awoke in Saint-Cyr to find himself under its wheels.

A certain laborer of Montmartre, named Fraire but called Cruddy, died of amazement, a newly made heir, in the office of a notary, Seine-et-Oise.

The solicitude of the Versailles police has been extended to seven derelicts who will sleep less badly in jail than in the train station.

Armed and dangerous, Thiercelin and Chapuis, now in the Pontois jail, robbed J. Maceron and P. Jean.

While grilling a pig, an apprentice set fire to the straw, and the slaughterhouse belonging to Vésinet butcher M. Cornu went up in smoke.

No, automobile 76 in the Gaillon race did not hit the mover's van, but was itself damaged, breaking a front wheel.

To have done with a stomach ailment, Mme Louis Normand, of Issou, hanged herself.

A soldier of the 40th Artillery Regiment assaulted, in the fields of Maizy, Meuse, a 60-year-old woman. He is being sought.

Four very beautiful pearls have been mysteriously stolen from the château of Gesvres-le-Duc, at Crouy-sur-Ourcq.

In the military zone, in the course of a duel over scrawny Adeline, basketweaver Capello stabbed bearbaiter Monari in the abdomen.

Yesterday afternoon, Henri Broussin was throwing stones at passersby on Rue de Paris in Montreuil. He is now in the workhouse infirmary.

About 100 waiters protested yesterday at six o'clock against two cafés, on Boulevard de Strasbourg and Rue Béranger.

Poupon, Gaudin, Jiffray, Ordronneau, and Granic all deny killing Mme Louet. The judge in Ramouillet had them arrested anyway.

The crime of Prunay-sous-Athis. It seems that Mme Faudoire's release is imminent, but not that of her husband.

Eighteen of 19 town councillors of Tournus, Saône-et-Loire, believe that parliamentarians are too highly paid and too numerous.

The matricide Gauthard, who was to have appeared
tomorrow before the assizes of Yonne, threw himself
out the window; he fractured his pelvis.

The *Virago* and other old cannons have been put aboard a
ship at Bordeaux, an English factory having bought them
for their bronze.

The money changer J. Banon was on the lam. Caught
near Digne, he was returned to Marseilles, site of his
illegal activities.

The prosecutor at Rambouillet ordered the arrest of Mme
Gaudoire, daughter of old Bellanger, who hanged himself
or was hanged by another.

Fire destroyed, in Crezieux, Loire, a house that the
Viscount of Meaux, a former minister of state, had filled
with rare antiques.

In the hamlet of Boutaresse, Puy de Dôme, widow Giron
was strangled, robbed, and hanged—by whom, no one
knows.

Surrounded by five gendarmes in the Vincennes villa
they were burglarizing, Lambert, Rives, and Liplet
surrendered.

At Toulouse, workers from all enterprises demonstrated
against the gas company, which is hostile to trade unions.

LE COUP DE VENT

Leaving the station at Vienne, Isère, the number 8
express ran over tracklayer Martel, a father of nine.

With a shot to the heart, the murderer of Mlle Hureux
killed himself in Lans, across the street from his family
home.

Over her protests, a soldier tossed Mlle Laveline, of
Nancy, back and forth on a swing a bit too vigorously.
A fatal drop of 12 feet.

The blow he struck on the sacriligious hands of an auditing
gendarme earned 20 days' jail to Le Nadan, a Breton from
Moustoir.

Lovers, Gilles, 24, of Piolenc, and an even younger
divorcée committed suicide in Orange by combined
means of poison and asphyxiation.

M. Jean-Baptiste Trystram, a former member of
Parliament and honorary president of the Chamber
of Commerce, died last night at eight o'clock.

With a cheese knife, Coste, from the suburbs of
Marseilles, killed his sister who, also a grocer, was
his competition.

At five o'clock, Marie Leca began her duties as maid at
the home of Dr. Metzger; at eight she left, taking 10,000
francs' worth of furs and gems.

When Mme Blood arrived in Toulouse on the 116 express, 36,000 francs' worth of jewels were allegedly missing from her trunks.

At the assizes of the Marne, the carter Vittet was sentenced to prison for life. He had killed Mayor Lelarge with four blows of a hammer.

Striking weavers at Lille threw mud at the director of their company. He fired without hitting anyone.

Latteux, of Saint-Ouen, fell into the emergency pipe of a hydrant that opens in the middle of the Seine. He drowned.

Caught in the act of breaking into a villa in Saint-Cloud, Le Marec, of Puteaux, and Desfays, of Nanterre, were arrested.

The investor Léopold Fleuriot, 60, who was hunting in the Sagy district, caught a volley point-blank.

On Rue Neuve-des-Boulets, homemaker Dumé, 42, of Rue de la Petite-Pierre, was plugged by a shot fired from no one knows where.

On the terrace of a wineshop on Quai des Fleurs, all the tables have been broken. The reason: to enforce the weekly day of rest.

Some people claiming to be Portuguese, who were perhaps not Portuguese, along with Mme de Bragance left Versailles, skipping out on her hotel.

Christian Doublier, 3, of Pantin, was fatally scalded when he fell into a laundry vat.

The Blonquets stank of drink. A saloonkeeper in Saint-Maur dared refuse them service. They slew him with an indignant dagger.

It was night. Of five persons traveling from Damvix to Arcais, three and the horse were drowned, the party having fallen into the river Sèvre.

The naval prefect of Brest was entertaining officers from the Russian squadron. One of them, chief warrant officer Gramozdine, died.

Two members of a track crew, hit by a stray train car, were crushed in the station at Rochefort.

In the lycée at Amiens was unveiled a plaque dedicated to Louis Thuillier, who died of cholera in Egypt, where he was studying.

Six prowlers—among them Tropenier, the leader—who were ravaging the henhouses, shop displays, and villas of Courbevoie, have been caught.

Mondier, of 75 *bis* Rue des Martyrs, was reading in bed. He set the sheets on fire, and now lies abed in Lariboisière hospital.

Young Guillemeau and Boileau have been arrested at Saint-Cloud while practicing their profession as burglars.

A poor box dedicated to St. Anthony of Padua was smashed in the church of St. Germain-l'Auxerrois. The saint is on the trail of the thief.

In front of 18 Rue Ampère, delivery coachman Jean Habon, 60, was crushed by his runaway carriage.

At the hospitals La Charité (Corvisart room) and Broussais (the laboratory) occurred fires that hurt no one.

In Oyonnax, Mlle Cottet, 18, threw acid in the face of M. Besnard, 25. Love, obviously.

Lalauze, 38, a shop assistant in Avignon, was killed in a bicycle accident at Montfavet, where he was collecting debt payments.

This time the crucifix is solidly bolted to the wall of the school at Bouillé. So much for the prefect of Maine-et-Loire.

The fairs of the region of Remiremont are closed to cattle, goats, sheep, and pigs due to hoof-and-mouth disease.

Overwhelmed by financial reversals, M. C., a bank employee, fractured his jaw with a gunshot in a thicket in the Bois de Boulogne.

With his ferret and his dog, investor Thiercelin, of Milly, went off hunting yesterday. He has not returned. The woods are being searched.

People were beginning to think the telegraph-cable thieves were supernatural. And yet one has been caught: Eugène Matifos, of Boulogne.

Headless and with his chest torn open, Arsius, 15, of Champigny, lay in a tunnel. A crime, it was believed. No, he had fallen from a train.

Mme Briotat, 71, of Vincennes, was burned alive (her lamp fell). At Charenton, little Magot's crib caught on fire.

Baron Jean de Christille, former diplomat. Under that name, Ferbet, arrested yesterday in Choisy-le-Roi, milked the peerage for 15 years.

The itinerant François Étienne, 22, who killed Louis Dallon, 18, at Estampes, was sentenced to eight years' hard time.

M. Lequeux brought before a vote of the town council of La Fère, Aisne, a formal protest against the greed of the legislator.

Seized near Belfort by five German customs agents, Ronfort made such a racket that they all ran home, exhausted.

It wasn't the mayor of Charmoille and his daughter who were arrested at their audit; it was the mayor of R., a nearby town, and *his* daughter.

Already the husband of Thérèse Hannot, Lhuilier of Pierry, Marne, last month married Maria Lourdeau. He was arrested for bigamy.

Rather than surrender his duties, M. Rey, of Saint-Calais, had barricaded himself in. The door was knocked down. He had vanished.

Colonel de Lestapis, of the 14th Hussars, has requested an early retirement. He is displeased that the churches are being audited.

Deciding that the 1906 amnesty applies to crimes and offenses ancillary to desertion, the military tribunal of Châlons acquitted Landucci.

The union at the Rochefort arsenal has decided to present four demands. And if they are refused? A strike.

The *Loire* is leaving from Aix island for Guyana on December 21 with a load of 490 convicts, of whom 265 are in for hard time.

Suicide by incineration: Mme Le Bise, of Landriec, Finistère, soaked her skirts with kerosene and set them alight.

Lefloch, Bataille, and Besnard had only gathered about a mile of telephone cable when, near Athis, they were arrested.

X. had put on an official cap. He could then cut at his leisure 8,700 feet of telephone cable along National Highway 19.

Burglary has befallen Montgeron, afflicting the villas of M. Loubière, M. Soulier, M. Petit, and M. Rayer.

Ordered to surrender, bootleggers who were landing a boatload of liquor at Boulogne swam away to safety instead.

A ruined Parisian merchant, Nicolas Darmont, hanged himself in Chatillon; left by his wife, Gineys, of Deuil, suffocated.

Bassinet, a ragpicker of Versailles, found 40,000 francs' worth of bonds and, just as in Mirbeau's *The Pocketbook*, gave them back.

After long being beaten by him, Fleur des Bastions obtained her revenge by pummeling with a knife the face of Gabriel Mélin, of Pantin.

The mayor of Vésinet cannot abide car horns. When they are in his jurisdiction they will have to remain silent.

Mlle Paulin, 46, of Mureaux, was assaulted, at nine in the evening, by a pervert (22, squat, felt hat, oval face).

At the home of Gabrielle Contret, whose charms are well-known in Lunéville, was seized an apparatus for counterfeiting Belgian écus.

The number 61 Nation-Dauphine metro hit Joseph Guérin, who had dropped his cane on the tracks and was trying to pick it up.

In the heat of an argument, hatmaker François Tondu knifed his father, Jean-Baptiste.

As touchy as a husband, Louis Dubé stabbed his mistress Florence Prévost on Rue de Flandre.

On Quai de la Conférence, two streetcars collided. Several passengers going from Gare de Lyon to Alma were slightly distressed.

A lost child (3 years old, blue suit) was found in tears last night on Place de la Bastille.

At 4:40 P.M., the 463 hit tracklayer Pierre Orillé, of Nanterre, in a tunnel, but did not kill him.

While leaving a dance hall in Aubervilliers, Jules Rivière stuck his dirk in Henri Brabant's back.

It took an enormous effort to bring down Bourlont and Vastelot, who were smashing shopfronts and molesting citizens in Charenton.

With no apparent motive, Virard, a coachman, selected the Dictuses of Gennevilliers as his target. One bullet struck the wife.

Night in Bas-Meudon. A temptress was luring Loret toward a den of passion when four brutes in slippers stripped him of everything.

The military dirigible *Patrie* made two free ascensions yesterday morning at Moisson, under the command of M. Voyer and M. Bois.

Robin and Cugnien were picked up, injured, in Versailles. Claimed to be victims of assault. Are thought to have been dueling with knives.

One man on Harbourg island and another aboard the drifting *Lardieu* sent out distress signals. A dinghy from Brest went to their assistance.

Accompanied by an old man, Jeanne Ostende, 18, entered a barracks in Toulon and knifed Victor Michel, a sailor.

The director of the streetcar lines in Brest, 63 times guilty of neglecting workers' breaks, will pay 63 fines of one franc.

The prefect of Finistère wanted to conduct audits at Molène and Ouessant, but the storm forced him to return to Brest.

A dispute between ragpickers in Saint-Ouen. After being hit by a cudgel wielded by Z. Mordiaz, Fromental brought an iron bar down on his neck.

Appointed by Napoleon, M. de Dion will tomorrow preside over a banquet on the anniversary of the election of L. Bonaparte to the head of the R.

Assisted by the storm, evildoers burglarized the church at Reynie, near Toulon, which was already hit three months ago.

Hélène Pook disliked being beaten. So she left Furth. But he encountered her at Porte d'Ivry and struck her this time with a knife.

Locked in the tramps' shelter in Bray, where their pipe set the pallet on fire, two peddlers were already roasted when the door was opened.

Marcelle, of Sèvres, had the investor Weiss in her bed and in her closet Julot, who left it, armed with a stiletto, and pocketed the gold.

For the fifth time Cuvillier, a fishmonger in Marines, has poisoned himself, and this time was definitive.

"Ouch!" cried the cunning oyster eater, "A pearl!" Someone at the next table bought it for 100 francs. It had cost 30 cents at the dime store.

Sailors at Viry-Châtillon fished out a very swollen Mme Hélène Merlin. She was neurasthenic, said her husband, whom she left a fortnight ago.

Around seven o'clock in the evening a few fripperies burned up in a costume shop, Place du Théâtre Français.

A fire at 162 Boulevard Voltaire. A fire captain was injured. Two brigadiers were hit on the head, one by a beam, the other by a fireman.

Rifleman Patureau, of the 111th Regiment at Toulon, died last night from the bullet he had accidentally lodged near his heart the previous day.

While on sentry duty Gustave Langlois, of the 4th Colonial Regiment, shot himself under the chin with his rifle. His head flew into bits.

Simply because they had restored the true God to the schools, the proconsul of Maine-et-Loire has persecuted another four mayors.

On Place Cambronne, an altercation between Raynouard, a pastry cook, and Louise Tumortier. She was shot twice in the thigh.

A fire at Orsay, at the Morin lumberyard. Two injuries; fireman Maurice and drummer Lacheny.

The harlots of Brest were selling illusions with the additional assistance of opium. At several houses the police seized gum and pipes.

In Maine-et-Loire the mayors never tire of rehanging the almighty on schoolroom walls, nor does the prefect tire of suspending their duties.

At Lyons, Pierre Melani, who killed police commissioner Montial, listened angrily as the death sentence was passed.

The chief commissioner of Perpignan was booed, hissed, and pelted with stones at Villelongue, where he was investigating an audit incident.

The widow Jules Morel, 72, of Arnas, Rhône, and of independent means, has been throttled. She was asleep when she was so treated.

"Why don't we migrate to Les Palaiseaux?" Yes, but M. Lencre, while enroute by cabriolet, was assaulted and robbed.

Deserted by Gomin, of La Croix-de-Berny, Juliette Droubly of Asnières tore up his mug with the points of her scissors.

Nineteen hundred contestants were fishing yesterday in the Sèvre, and 15,000 spectators were encouraging the fish to bite.

# ILLUSTRATIONS

# ILLUSTRATIONS

# ILLUSTRATIONS

# OTHER NEW YORK REVIEW BOOKS CLASSICS*

\* *For a complete list of titles, visit www.nyrb.com or write to:*
 *Catalog Requests, NYRB, 1755 Broadway, New York, NY 10009-3780*